Reader's Digest
Energy-Efficient
Home Manual

Reader's Digest
Energy-Efficient
Home Manual

Expert guidance on saving energy and conserving water

Published by
The Reader's Digest Association Limited
London • New York • Sydney • Montreal

Contents

Introduction

6   About this book

The energy-efficient home

10   How efficient is your home?

Saving energy

14   Top ten ways to conserve energy
18   Room-by-room guide to saving electricity
19   Smart lighting solutions
24   Generating power
27   Grants for improving your home's efficiency
28   Making home improvements

Insulation and ventilation

32   Insulation and ventilation

Double glazing

33   Choosing double glazing
34   Replacing double-glazed panes
35   Secondary double glazing

Draughtproofing

38   Windows
41   Doors
43   Floors

Insulation

45   Insulating your home
46   Lofts and roofs
50   Walls
54   Pipes

Heating

58   Heating options
60   Saving heat
62   Heating water

Central heating

65   Installation
67   Maintenance
68   Controlling your central heating
70   Choosing radiators and other heat emitters
73   Boilers
75   Hot-water cylinders
77   Immersion heaters
80   Radiators

Conserving water

90   Saving water around the home
95   Repairs to leaking pipes and taps
105   Repairing and replacing a WC

Collecting and recycling water

110   Installing guttering
115   Gutter maintenance
120   Collecting rainwater and grey water

123   **Products and suppliers**
125   **Index**
128   **Acknowledgments**

About this book

Whether you want to save money on your fuel and water bills or want to do your bit to save the planet, cutting down on the energy and water used in the home is a topic on everyone's mind. This book will help you to assess the efficiency of your home and gives you tips and step-by-step instructions for improving it.

Improving the energy-efficiency of your home is not just about saving money on bills. All homes now require an Energy Performance Certificate (see page 13) as part of the Home Information Pack that a vendor must compile when selling. Equipping your home with energy-saving measures – whether it's switching to low-energy compact fluorescent tube light bulbs throughout the house or installing solar panels on your roof for heating water – will help to improve the rating your house is given and can help to make your property more attractive to potential purchasers.

See the heat escape A thermal image shows where this house is efficiently insulated (the roof) and where it is not (the windows).

How green is your home?

Chapter One, The energy-efficient home, takes you through each major element of your home – windows, doors, walls, roof and more – and helps you to assess their energy-efficiency. You'll find the top ten ways to conserve energy, from drying your washing on the line rather than in the tumble dryer to making sure that all your hot-water pipes and tanks are lagged to keep as much of the heat as possible inside. Did you know that fitting draught excluders around all the doors and opening windows in the house can cut heat loss by as much as 25 per cent in winter? Or that insulating cavity walls could save you up to £160 a year on your heating costs? Turn to pages 14–17 to find out more.

For many of us, the electricity bill is often the biggest shock when it arrives. Pages 18–23 take you room-by-room around the house with great tips for cutting down your electricity consumption. Only boil as much water as you really need to use, always turn off the television at the set – leaving it on stand-by still drains a surprising amount of power – remember to switch off the lights when you leave a room and fit a PIR sensor to your front-door light so that it only comes on when you need it: when someone approaches. These and other simple tips are easy to follow and can all add up to big savings. If you want to go even further, you'll find all you need to know about using solar panels and wind turbines to generate some of your own electricity on pages 24–26 and helpful advice on some of the grants that are available for installing energy-saving measures on page 27. And pages 28–29 will help you to make any home improvements or extensions energy-wise.

Keep the heat in

Thermal images, like the one opposite, show the parts of a house where heat escapes the most. In this house, the windows are 'white hot' and may be only single-glazed, heat is radiating from red hot walls – perhaps hard-to-insulate solid brick or uninsulated cavity walls – but insulation in the loft is keeping the roof cool and preventing heat from escaping upwards.

Chapter Two, Insulation and ventilation, is full of advice and clear step-by-step instructions for improving your home's insulation – in walls, roofs and floors or with double glazing. You'll find illustrated instructions for lagging pipes, draught-proofing doors and windows and topping up the insulation in your loft if you have less than the recommended depth of 270mm. Find out more on pages 32–55.

Use your heating wisely

Understanding how your central heating and hot-water systems work and using them wisely is the most effective way to make the best use of the heat they generate. Chapter Three, Heating, explains the different methods of heating rooms and water and helps you to evaluate the many options. You'll find out how solar panels for heating water can make a big difference to your heating bills, even in gloomy Britain, on page 64 and how the position of your radiators can make a difference to their efficiency on page 66. You'll find tips on choosing the most efficient radiators, boilers, hot-water cylinders and more; maintenance advice to keep them working efficiently and step-by-step instructions for repairs when things go wrong. See pages 58–87 to find out more.

Top tips for conserving water

With summer hosepipe bans becoming an annual feature in many parts of the country and a growing awareness of the scarcity of this most vital resource, water is something that we should never take for granted. Chapter Four, Conserving water, will help you to limit your water usage around the home and show you how to collect rainwater or grey water from within the house to use where drinking-quality water from the mains is not essential.

Pages 90–94 are packed with water-saving tips – like replacing a standard, old-fashioned WC with a modern slimline model that uses half the amount of water for each flush, or switching your old showerhead for a new 'champagne' aerated head that could save you up to 50,000 litres of water a year – and a few surprising facts. Did you know that a five-minute power shower can use at least as much water as a soak in the tub? It may be a time-saver, but showering is not necessarily the most water-wise option. There's advice on choosing appliances that use less water and on using water carefully in the garden by watering at the right time of day and mulching beds to lock in the moisture.

You'll also find easy-to-follow step-by-step instructions for fixing burst pipes and dripping taps – a dripping tap left unattended to can waste as much as 140 litres of water in a week – that's a whole bathful – and if it's a hot tap you'll be wasting energy heating water that is dripping straight down the drain, too. Turn to pages 98–104 and stop wasting water now.

Another great way to ease the demands on the mains water system is to collect as much rainwater as you can. Pages 110–119 tell you everything you need to know about guttering and downpipes to harvest rainwater from your house, garage and even the garden shed. Pages 120–123 then show you how to fit water butts to store it and explain all about larger rainwater tanks and the options for collecting 'grey water' from baths, washing macines and basins to use in the garden or even to route back into the house for flushing toilets or washing the car. See what *you* can do to make a difference.

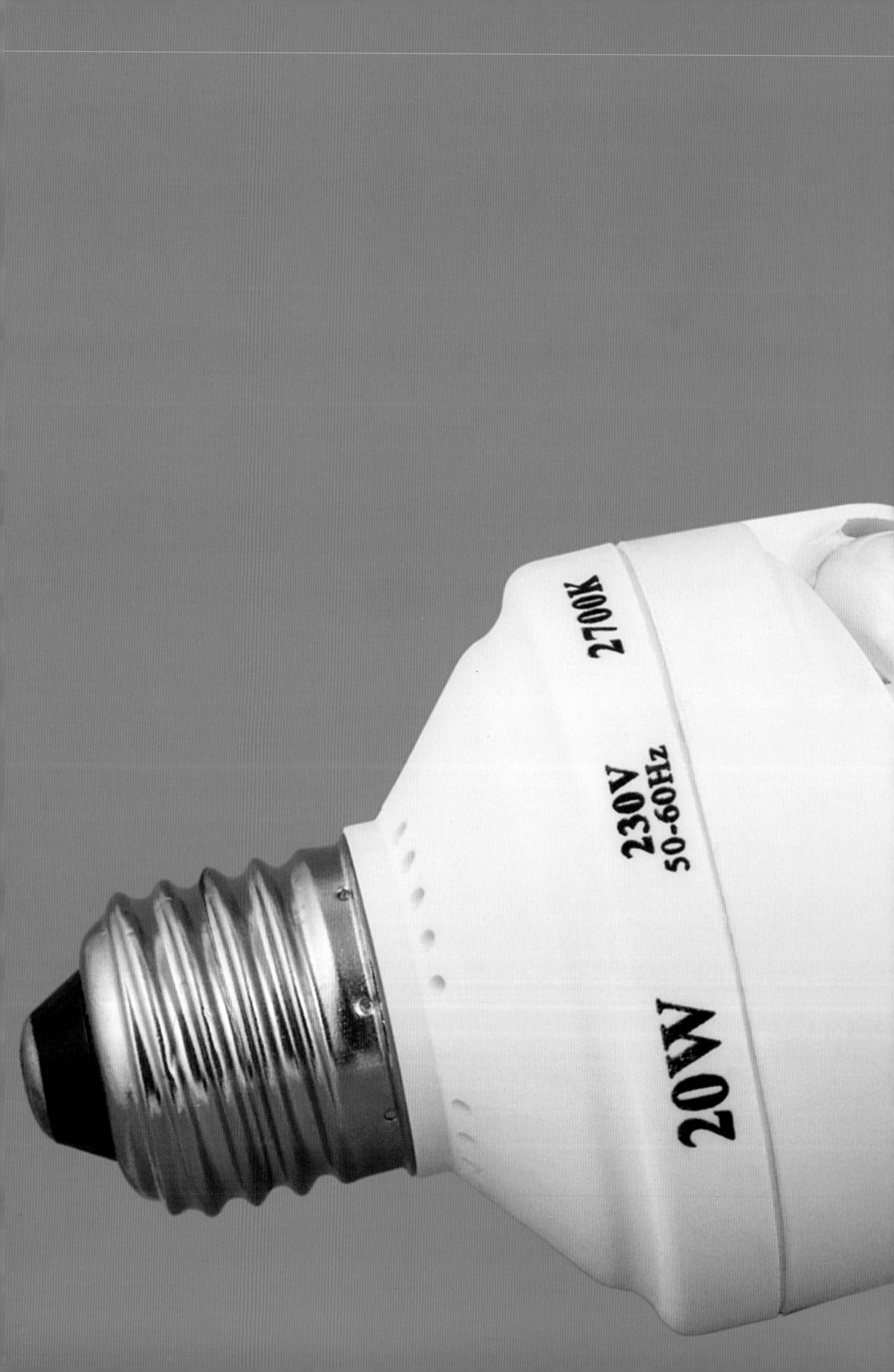
2700K
230V
50-60Hz
20W

The energy-efficient home

How efficient is your home?

A house that uses energy inefficiently, by allowing heat to escape through a poorly insulated loft, for example, will be expensive to run. As part of the new Home Information Packs, all houses for sale are assessed and given an energy rating. This chapter shows you what you can do to give your house the best possible rating.

The first step is to assess your home's energy efficiency and identify its weak points. Start by considering the age and construction of your home. A new home with cavity walls, floor insulation and other energy-saving measures that has been constructed to the latest Building Regulations requirements will, of course, be more energy-efficient than a Victorian property with draughty wooden floorboards and solid brick walls.

You cannot change the fabric of your home, but once you understand what you have you can work within those limits to make improvements where you can and reduce the amount of energy you use.

Windows and doors

Look closely at all the windows and doors in the house. Single-glazed windows are the least efficient insulators, and doors and windows with wooden frames are prone to rot and gaps. Any old windows or doors with decaying frames that may be draughty should be replaced.

If windows are double-glazed, check the size of the gap between the panes – the larger the gap, the better the insulation the window will provide. All new windows must comply with Part L (conservation of fuel and power) of the Building Regulations

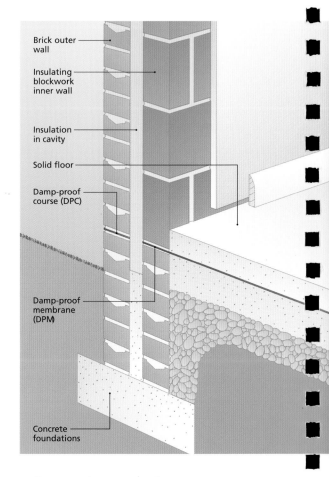

Brick outer wall

Insulating blockwork inner wall

Insulation in cavity

Solid floor

Damp-proof course (DPC)

Damp-proof membrane (DPM)

Concrete foundations

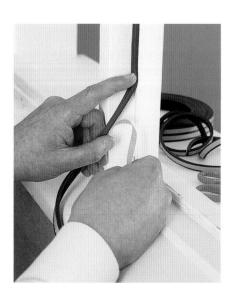

so if you are planning to replace any windows ask your supplier for advice.

Finally, make sure that all windows and doors are fitted with appropriate draught excluders to keep in as much precious heat as possible.

Walls

Consider how the walls of your home are constructed. Cavity walls (above) provide the best insulation, particularly if the cavity has been filled with insulating material. The walls may be a double skin of brick or brick on the outside and concrete blocks inside, but both methods are effective insulators.

Solid walls heat up on the inside and allow the heat to radiate from the outside, making them much less effective at keeping

heat in. There are options for insulating solid walls (see page 14), so check to see whether your walls have been clad with insulation.

Roof and loft
All lofts should be well insulated, although it is also important to allow a little ventilation into the roof space to prevent damp forming. Check the thickness of any loft insulation. If your loft is not currently insulated, installing a 270mm thickness of insulation (the standard required by Building Regulations in new builds) across the whole area could cut your bills by up to a third. Topping up existing insulation to at least 250mm deep will also help and some grants are available to help with the work. Your own energy provider may also have a scheme providing discounts to encourage customers to fit adequate loft insulation.

Lights
Take stock of the light bulbs in use around the house and assess how many are traditional incandescent bulbs and how many are energy-saving compact fluorescent lamps (see page 16). Consider, too, whether you have rooms lit by multiple light fittings and whether they are all necessary – a bank of spotlights, even low-energy ones, is a more wasteful method of lighting a room than a single pendant light fitting with an appropriate wattage of low-energy bulb fitted.

Replacing all the bulbs in a house at once can be a costly exercise, but buy a selection of low-energy bulbs and fit them in place of standard bulbs each time an existing bulb blows.

Hot water
Find and inspect your hot-water tank and as many exposed hot-water pipes as you can. Pipes should be lagged either with a fibre bandage wrapped around them or, better still, lengths of foam that clip around the pipes (below). Most modern hot water

cylinders have a hard coat of sprayed-on lagging – tap the cylinder to see whether it feels solid. If you have a bare metal cylinder, wrap it in a lagging jacket immediately (see page 61).

A very efficient system for heating water is to use solar panels, which may be installed on the roof of the house or of a convenient outbuilding.

Central heating

The central heating system is one of the main energy users in the home and your boiler is the powerhouse, so it is important to assess what type you have and how efficiently it works.

The most efficient type of boiler is a condensing boiler. These are expensive to fit, but over their lifetime you will more than recoup that cost in savings, particularly if you are planning to remain in a house for some years. If your boiler needs replacing always try to choose a condensing type.

Look at the central heating controls, too. At the least, you should have a timed controller and a thermostat in one room. If the thermostat is positioned opposite a fire or in another warm place it will turn off the heating before the rest of the house is warm enough and you will find yourself turning up the temperature across the whole house to compensate. Consider how

> ## REGULATIONS
>
> Replacing a boiler, installing new windows and inserting cavity wall insulation are all categories of work that are subject to Building Regulations control. If you are uncertain whether you need approval for work you are planning, call your local council's Building Control Officer for advice.

you use your house, whether you are at work during the day, and whether there are elderly people or young children in the family, who may need the temperature to be a little warmer. Many programmers allow you to set a different heating schedule for weekdays and weekends. The most efficient types allow you to specify different temperatures at different times of day (see page 16).

For maximum efficiency, combine a single main room thermostat with individual thermostatic radiator valves (TRVs) (below). This way, each room can be controlled separately.

THE ENERGY PERFORMANCE CERTIFICATE

By 2008, European Law stipulates that every home sold in the EU must have an EPC, or Energy Performance Certificate. Here, this is already a requirement of the Home Information Packs that must be compiled by homeowners before putting their property on the market. The EPC uses the government-approved Standard Assessment Procedure (SAP) to assess the energy-efficiency of a property and to gauge its environmental impact in terms of CO_2 emissions. The report considers the building itself, any fixed appliances within it and the use of energy-saving devices, such as compact fluorescent light bulbs and thermostatic radiator valves throughout. Energy-saving additions and home improvements, such as solar panels for heating water or generating energy, will also be taken into account. The more energy-efficient the home the higher the SAP rating, which promises potential purchasers lower fuel bills and reduced carbon emissions.

The Home Information Pack's EPC will rate a property on a 120-point scale, divided into seven categories . These range from A (most efficient) to G (least efficient) – this is the same A-G scale that is used to rate electrical appliances, such as washing machines, dishwashers and fridges. The survey takes less than an hour for an average home and should cost around £150.

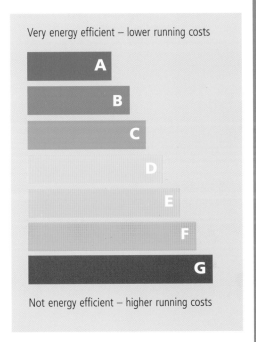

Very energy efficient – lower running costs

A
B
C
D
E
F
G

Not energy efficient – higher running costs

Where appropriate, the Home Information Pack will recommend measures that can be taken to increase the property's efficiency. These are graded by cost of installation and potential cost savings in reduced energy use over a period of 10 years. Only major works, such as replacing an old boiler with a new, more efficient one, are likely to raise your property from one banding to a higher one, but even simple things like replacing incandescent light bulbs with low-energy compact fluorescent tubes will make a difference to your rating.

Why take note of the energy rating?

Over time, heating and lighting an inefficient property will cost considerably more than running a home that is well insulated and fitted with energy-saving devices. So when you are buying a new home is it worth comparing the energy ratings of the properties you are considering and, if necessary, assessing the cost of improving them. Likewise, you may be able to improve the saleability of your home by doing all you can to raise its rating. The advice in this book will help you to assess your home, identify places where improvements could be made and to carry out the necessary work confidently and successfully.

Better efficiency means lower bills

Even if you are not buying or selling a house, there are many simple things you can do that will reduce your energy bills. Your gas or electricity provider may also have an online survey you could complete that will give you an energy rating and suggest low cost, higher cost and more significant upgrades and improvements that you could consider undertaking.

Top ten ways to conserve energy

It doesn't have to be difficult to cut down the amount of energy you use in your home. Here are ten simple tips for being energy-aware.

Almost half of the UK's carbon dioxide emissions come from producing the energy we use each day, so anything you can do to reduce your household energy consumption will help towards minimising the production of these damaging greenhouse gases.

Insulate

Good insulation will not only help to keep your home warm in winter, minimising your heating bills, but it will also stay cool in summer, reducing the need for electric fans or air conditioning units. A well-insulated home can be as much as 10°C warmer in winter and 7°C cooler in summer than a non-insulated equivalent house. Walls, floors, lofts and windows can all be insulated.

If you have cavity walls, make sure that they are insulated. Cavity wall insulation can save up to £160 a year on heating costs – and you may be eligible for a grant towards the installation costs.

AVOID WASTING HOT WATER

Every time you turn on the hot tap, up to 1 litre or more of cold water is drawn out through the pipe before the water begins to run hot.

For washing your hands or many other quick jobs you will often have finished before the hot water comes through, but it will still have been drawn out of the hot-water tank. The hot water will cool again in the pipe until you next turn on the tap while the topped-up tank is heated back to the set temperature.

Use the cold tap whenever possible to avoid wasting energy heating water that will not get used.

Solid walls are harder and more expensive to insulate, but they can be covered, either inside or outside, with a layer of insulating material. In practice, this is most feasible if you are undertaking a major renovation project and can insulate the walls on the inside as you gut and refit each individual room. Bear in mind that the rooms will be made slightly smaller by the thickness of the insulation and the battens used to fix them in place if necessary on each external wall.

To find out more about double glazing see pages 33–37 and to discover the secrets of insulating your home's loft, roof and walls, turn to pages 45–53.

Close the curtains

Even draught-proofed, double-glazed windows will lose some heat, particularly in winter, when temperatures outside are low – they can contribute up to 20 per cent of

the total heat loss from a home. Hanging good quality, heavy, lined curtains that fit snugly to the wall and have a closed pelmet at the top could reduce heat loss by up to a third.

Stop any gaps

Use draught excluders to plug any gaps around doors, windows, letterboxes or any other external openings to prevent heat escaping. Even keyholes can be sealed with a simple escutcheon plate that swings out of the way when you need to unlock the door. Fitting draught excluders all round your home could cut heat loss by up to 25 per cent in winter. Follow the easy steps to draught-proofing your home on pages 38–44.

HOUSEHOLD ENERGY USE

More than half of the energy used in an average home goes on heating the house and the hot water. Any energy-saving measures implemented in these areas will have a big impact in reducing the overall energy consumption – and the fuel bills, too.

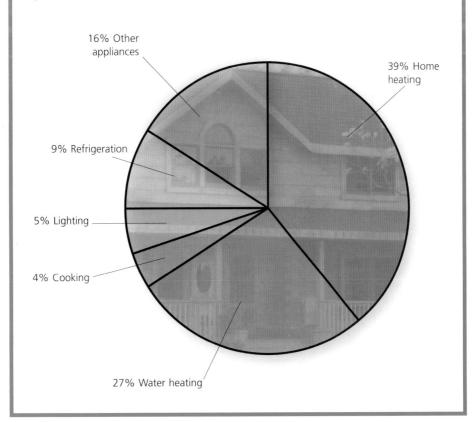

16% Other appliances

39% Home heating

9% Refrigeration

5% Lighting

4% Cooking

27% Water heating

DON'T HEAT EMPTY ROOMS

If there are rooms in your house that you don't use on a regular basis, such as a spare bedroom, turn off the radiator and close the door. They will soon warm up again if you have guests coming to stay and you won't waste energy – and money – heating rooms unnecessarily.

Lag tanks and pipes

Make sure that all hot-water tanks and exposed pipes are well insulated with specialist lagging. As much as half of the total water-heating costs in an average home can be attributed to heat lost through poor insulation of pipes and tanks. A lagging jacket for a bare metal hot-water cylinder can cost as little as £10 but will reduce heat loss by 75 per cent, making your water heating instantly more efficient. Find out how to lag water pipes on pages 54–55 and follow the other heat-saving tips on page 61.

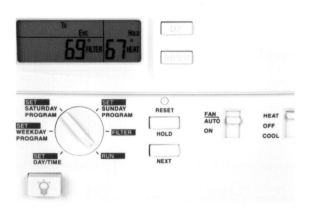

Turn down the heat

You can turn down the temperature on your central heating thermostat by 1° and not notice the difference in the house – but you may save up to 10 per cent on your heating bills.

If you don't already have one, fit a digital thermostat that will enable you to control the heating more precisely – even better is a digital programmable thermostat (above) that allows you to set the heating to different temperatures for different times of day, so that you are not heating rooms unnecessarily or to a higher temperature than you really need. Find out how to upgrade your programmer on page 69.

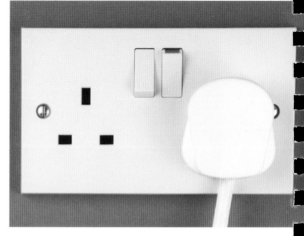

Switch off at the wall

Leaving your television, video or even microwave on 'stand-by' when you're not using it can account for 10 per cent of a household's electricity bill.

Repeatedly switching off and on something you use often will prove irritating and even the most dedicated energy saver is unlikely to stick to the regime, but always switch off appliances at the wall if you are not going to be using them again for more than a couple of hours and definitely do it over night.

Use low-energy light bulbs

Replace standard incandescent light bulbs with low-energy compact fluorescent lamps (CFLs). Energy-saving light bulbs last between 6 and 15 times longer than standard bulbs and use 80 per cent less electricity. Replacing a standard 100W light bulb with a 20W low energy light bulb can save around £12 per year in electricity costs. They are available in a wide range of styles and wattages to suit all kinds of lamps and fittings.

Dry clothes outside

Even the most efficient tumble driers are hungry consumers of electricity. Whenever the weather allows, use an outdoor clothes line for drying your washing. For low-energy drying on wet days, consider whether you have room to install a permanent drying rack in a utility room or other room inside the house.

Choose gas over electricity

If you have a choice between gas and electricity for cooking or heating, choose gas. It is usually cheaper and a more efficient form of energy, but is also far kinder to the environment. Providing gas to domestic users produces one third of the greenhouse gas emissions that a coal-fired power station would produce to generate an equivalent amount of electricity.

Choose appliances wisely

Always look for energy-efficient options when buying new home appliances – all appliances are energy-rated, with A+ or A++ being the most energy-efficient. Ask whether an appliance is Energy Saving Recommended and look out for the Energy Saving Trust logo (below) on appliances that are rated most efficient.

energy saving trust

It's not enough just to choose energy-efficient appliances, though. Make sure you choose ones that are appropriate for your needs – if you are a small household do not pick a large-capacity washing machine or an American-style refrigerator, that has much more room than you need. A 284-litre fridge will use 20 per cent more energy than a 210-litre fridge, even if they both have the same energy rating.

WASH CLOTHES AT A LOWER TEMPERATURE

Modern washing powders and liquids are just as effective at lower temperatures as their predecessors were in hot water. There is rarely any need for the boil wash of old and for most normal washing and common stains a much cooler wash will do perfectly well. Set your washing machine to a 30° cycle, rather than washing at 60° and you will use around 40 per cent less electricity for each load of laundry.

Room-by-room guide to saving electricity

Once you've addressed our top ten energy savers, don't stop there. Try some of these simple electricity-wise tips and techniques around the house to cut your bill even further.

Top tips in the Kitchen

Cup-by-cup
It may be obvious, but few of us do it: only boil as much water as you need each time you make a cup of tea. Most kettles have a water gauge on the side or in the handle, making it easy to see how many cupfuls of water are inside. Get into the habit of paying attention and not over-filling the kettle. The eco-kettle (above) makes it easy to measure out the right amount. A clever feature allows you to fill a reservoir inside the kettle then only allow the precise amount you need through to a separate chamber where the water is heated.

Cooker conservation
Many recipes begin with the instruction to preheat the oven before even starting to prepare the dish to go in it, but is it really necessary? Modern fan-assisted ovens heat up quickly and get to the required recipe temperature fast enough to make pre-heating a thing of the past, so don't waste energy by having your oven on when there is nothing cooking inside.

Whenever you use your oven do your best to do so efficiently. Rather than cooking one small dish at a time, think ahead and cook several things at once or find ways to cook accompaniments alongside the main dish in the oven, rather than on the stove top – roasting vegetables and potatoes instead of boiling them, for example.

Make the most of your microwave
Faster cooking times means less energy used. If you have a microwave, use it! There are hundreds of time and energy-saving uses for the microwave beyond simply reheating leftovers or cooking ready-meals. A baked potato, for example, can cook in 10 minutes, compared with more than an hour in a conventional oven, so think 'microwave' before you turn on the cooker.

Think small
Many small appliances around the kitchen, not just the microwave, are more energy-efficient than their equivalent function in the conventional oven. Using a toaster will generate one quarter of the greenhouse emissions produced by using an electric grill to cook your toast.

SMART LIGHTING SOLUTIONS FOR SAVING ENERGY

Turn them off when you leave

The single most important – and the simplest – thing you can do to cut down on energy wasted through lighting is to turn off the lights when you leave a room. Making best use of natural light will help to reduce the need for switching on lights in the first instance, so open blinds and curtains wide during daylight hours to let in as much light as possible and brighten dark rooms by decorating in light colours and using mirrors to reflect natural light. Position desks and working areas in other rooms, such as kitchen worktops, where there is good natural light and consider installing sky lights or sunlight pipes (see page 21) to improve the light in dark hallways or rooms without windows.

How many lights do you need?

Recessed halogen spotlights are a stylish option particularly popular in kitchens and bathrooms, but even the low-energy bulbs and fittings can be costly to run when fitted in the large numbers required to illuminate a whole room. If you plan to install recessed spotlights, seek out the fluorescent models that are now available.

Switch to low energy

Wherever possible, replace standard incandescent light bulbs with low-energy fluorescent alternatives. These are now available in a wide range of shapes, sizes, wattages and even 'tones' of light, with bayonet and screw fittings, so you will find a suitable bulb for most pendant and lamp fittings. They last up to 10 times longer and use around 80 per cent less electricity than an equivalent incandescent bulb. On average, compact fluorescent bulbs will pay for themselves in savings in about a year and a half and at least twice again over their lifetime. Low-energy bulbs do take a few seconds to warm up to full strength and frequent switching on and off can shorten their lifespan, so for rooms where you need a quick burst of light, such as a downstairs WC or under-stairs cupboard, you may prefer to retain a traditional bulb, but try to keep these exceptions to a minimum.

Ditch the dimmer

If you have a dimmer switch in a room and find that, more often than not, you use it dimmed, then replace the bulb with one of a lower wattage and go back to a conventional 'on or off' switch.

Dimmer switches might reduce the light level in a room but they do little to reduce the electricity that is used and there are very limited options for fitting low-energy bulbs in rooms controlled by a dimmer switch. Replacing a standard 100W bulb with a 40W for a low level of lighting will save 60 per cent of its running cost.

Top tips in the Living Room

Heating the room

Electric fires or radiant heaters are not efficient users of energy, but in some situations, where it is impossible to run a gas pipe into the living room they are the only available option for augmenting the heat from the central heating system.

First of all, consider whether you really need this extra heater. If you have central heating, could you fit a thermostatic radiator valve to the living room radiator and use this to raise the temperature in the room if it feels uncomfortably chilly for sitting still? If the electric fire is your only heat source, consider whether it is worth the expense and upheaval of installing gas-fired central heating – gas is a much more efficient fuel to use and uses much less energy to generate.

Electric storage heaters are another option where a gas supply is not available, and are more energy-efficient than a radiant bar or electric fan heater. They make use of cheaper off-peak electricity where available, and the most sophisticated models monitor the inside and sometimes the outside temperature and regulate their own temperature, and therefore their energy use, accordingly.

Stand by for big savings

The living room is often the room in the house with the most energy-guzzling appliances. Television, DVD player, digital television box, video recorder, stereo system, games console and computer are all plugged in around the room. Always turn them off at the plug when you've finished using them – although hard disc digital television recorders need to be left on to record programmes when you are not watching – rather than leaving them on 'stand-by' (see page 16).

Low lights, high cost

An effective way to create a relaxed atmosphere in a living room is to use low-level table lights rather than central pendant light fittings. A network of lamps can be wired into a lighting circuit that allows you to turn all the lamps on or off with a single flick of a switch. While this is an appealing look for a room, it does mean that lamps may often be switched on unnecessarily – if there is only one person in the room, needing just one lamp for reading, the others will also be burning needlessly.

You can, of course, still switch off individual lamps in a circuit by using the switch on the lamps themselves, but you

will need to be really committed to saving electricity to make this extra effort. A better energy-wise option is the old-fashioned method of operating lamps individually and only turning on the ones you need each time. Don't forget to fit low-energy light bulbs in your table lamps as well as the main light fittings in the room.

Top tips in the Bathroom

Choose automatic ventilation

An extractor fan is a valuable addition to a bathroom and is a requirement of the Building Regulations when installing a new bathroom in your home. These simple electric fans help to remove damp air that can lead to condensation and, to do this effectively, they need to run for longer than the time you are likely to spend in the room after you have finished your bath or shower. Leaving a manually operated fan running means that you must remember to go back to switch it off later to avoid wasting power after the moisture in the room has cleared.

A common alternative is a fan wired into the room's light switch, which comes on when the light is turned on and runs on a timer for a specified period after the light has been turned off. These fans can be turned off independently if need be, but are designed to come on whenever the room is used, so they will operate even when they are not needed to extract moist air. A better option is to fit a fan with a humidity sensor, which will come on automatically when the moisture levels in the room exceed the set level and will turn itself off once the humidity drops back down again.

Always make sure that you choose an extractor fan designed for use in a bathroom and one that is powerful enough for your room size.

Don't leave the light on

Regulations governing the use of light switches in a bathroom have led to the development of motion-sensitive light switches as an alternative to a pull-cord or a conventional switch located outside the room. These switches detect the movement of someone entering the room and turn on the light for a specified length of time. They are most suitable for separate WCs, where you are unlikely to spend much time and where it is easy to forget to switch off the light when you leave. In a bathroom where you may wish to relax with a long soak in the bath, there is a risk of the light turning off and plunging you into darkness, although you would only have to make some movement to switch it back on again.

Use hot water wisely

An electric immersion heater (see page 62) provides an excellent emergency back-up when you run out of hot water, and is usually fitted inside the main hot-water tank to top up the water temperature when needed. As with all heating devices, electricity is an inefficient power source, so relying on an immersion heater for all your hot water is a wasteful and expensive option. If you turn your immersion heater on, always remember to turn it back off again once it has done its job – most are manually operated, and it is easy to forget if the switch is hidden in an airing cupboard or other out-of-the-way place. To minimise the need for an immersion heater, make sure that your hot-water tank is an adequate size for your household's use. To maintain the temperature of the water inside for as long as possible, ensure that it is fitted with a lagging jacket if it does not have its own integral insulation. Time the water-heating cycle of your system to provide a full tank of hot water ready for the time or times of day when you use it most.

Modern, well-insulated cylinders should hold their temperature well for a whole day, but you may need a short second burst of heat to bring the tank back to temperature after it has refilled to replenish the water taken for morning showers.

SUNLIGHT PIPES

An ingenious and environmentally sound way to provide light and air to an internal, windowless bathroom or shower room is the sunlight pipe. Known as Sola-vent, the system consists of a sun pipe, a solar-powered fan and two low voltage 50W halogen lights, all housed in one unit. The unit combines solar powered ventilation and natural daylight from the rooftop and is effective even under overcast skies. A light catching prism on the roof, and a sun pipe with a highly reflective lining, bring natural light into the room during daylight hours. A motion sensor automatically switches on an extractor fan when someone goes into the bathroom, so there is no need for a manual switch. The low maintenance fan unit has been designed to be as quiet and unintrusive as possible. The unit complies with current Building Regulations. (For more information, visit www.sunpipe.co.uk)

Top tips in the Bedroom

Switch off before you fall asleep

It sounds obvious, but falling asleep with the light, radio or television on is easy to do and a clear waste of electricity. Many people have a television in the bedroom, and particularly in teenage children's bedrooms, and even if you remember to turn it off before switching out the light, once you are warm in bed it is tempting to stay put and leave the set on stand-by over night. Don't. Always get up to turn the television off at the set and make sure that other family members do the same.

If you have older children with rooms full of electronic gadgetry and energy-sapping entertainment systems try to involve them in the family's energy-saving efforts and encourage them to be mindful of their energy use.

Night lights

Try to get children used to sleeping in a dark room so that you do not always have to leave a light on in or outside the room. If you do use a night light, choose a battery-operated model that can be powered with rechargeable batteries or one that has a timer option. Touch-on-touch-off lights are easy to operate in the dark – better than leaving a night light always on – and will provide sufficient light when going into a child's room at night without using the main light.

Will a clockwork clock do?

A clock radio is on all day and night to power the clock, even though it is little

used during the day and seldom needed through the night. Think about whether a conventional wind-up or battery-operated bedside clock will meet your needs just as well, together with a radio that you can switch on separately when you wake up. Don't run clock radios or electrically powered clocks in spare bedrooms when they are not in use. Turn them on and set the time before your guests arrive and then switch them off again when they leave.

Top tips in the Hall

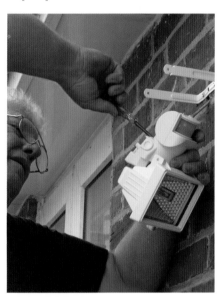

Don't light up the street

For safety, it is important to be able to see visitors who call at your front door when it is dark. It is also a good idea to illuminate your door for your own safety and comfort when coming home late at night. If you want to check through a spy hole before opening the door then you will need an outdoor light, and to check on your visitor furtively this will need to be switched on when they approach. There are two energy-saving alternatives to a straightforward outdoor light that is permanently switched on or that you switch on yourself as darkness falls. Whichever option you choose, try to fit an energy-saving bulb or look for light fittings that will accept one.

A dusk-to-dawn light has a light sensor, which switches the light on when ambient light levels dip below a specified level. Some stay on until dawn; others can be set to stay on for a specified length of time, which can be adjusted as nights draw in earlier, so that they switch themselves off around the time you usually go to bed. Many security lights are activated by a PIR

sensor, which detects visitors approaching the door and switches on for a short, pre-determined length of time. When setting up the light, experiment to find the best angle and position for the sensor so that it does not switch on the light every time someone passes by on the pavement.

Christmas lights

It may be festive to deck your house – inside and out – with brightly coloured lights at Christmas, but consider the cost of keeping them alight before you let yourself get carried away. The first and most important thing you can do is to run your lights from a timer switch, limiting their use so that they come on as dusk approaches and go off when you go to bed. Better still, only turn on indoor lights when you are in the room and can actually see them.

An even more effective way to save energy is to replace your conventional fairy lights with a string of low-energy LED bulbs. Like incandescent bulbs, these are available in a range of colours and string lengths, but the big difference is that each bulb uses only 0.04 watts each hour, making it 90 per cent more efficient than the equivalent incandescent bulb, and will last for 200,000 hours – or 23 years of continuous use.

Stair safety at night

If you have children or other family members who get up to use the bathroom at night, it is tempting to leave the landing light on to prevent accidental trips or falls down the stairs. Even with a low-energy lightbulb, it is wasteful powering a light all night long for an occasional use. If you don't want to disturb other members of the household by switching on the landing light, you could equip everyone with a bedside torch.

Alternatively, run a table lamp – equipped with a low-energy bulb – from a timer switch or, better still a dusk-to-dawn switch that will automatically turn it off when the ambient light is bright enough not to need it. Night lights that plug directly into a socket – usually sold alongside child safety equipment – are a simple solution that will also use less electricity than running a ceiling or table light.

A new development is the Safe-T-Light, a night light that plugs into a socket and gives low-level, low-energy lighting during hours of darkness and can also be detached for use as a rechargeable torch when necessary or in a power cut.

Home-made power

Generating some of your own electricity is a great way to reduce your reliance on power supplied from the National Grid, cutting down your bill and reducing the need for electricity to be generated commercially at the same time.

Solar power from photovoltaic (PV) cells and electricity generated by domestic wind turbines are all still in their infancy in the domestic and DIY market. There is a limit to what a DIY installation can hope to achieve and even a new house built with a home micro-power-generation system in mind is unlikely to be fully self-sufficient, but any power you can generate yourself can be used in place of paid-for electricity supplied via the National Grid.

Both systems have high initial set-up costs – both in the purchase of the equipment and in professional fitting costs, since few systems are designed for DIY installation – and it will be many years before you recoup the cost in savings on your electricity bill. But they are an investment in your home, will contribute towards a good rating on the property's energy performance certificate (EPC) – now required by law when you come to sell – and may help to make your house more

attractive to potential buyers. Whether or not your personal finances benefit, you will be making a positive contribution towards reducing your carbon footprint and lessening the western world's reliance on fossil fuels.

Solar panels for heating water are now more established and much more efficient; for more information, see page 64.

Solar panels

Panels of photovoltaic cells, commonly mounted on the house roof, transform the energy captured from sunlight into electricity for use in the home. The simplest systems are used to power a particular appliance or lighting point, that can be switched over to your conventional electricity supply if necessary.

Choosing solar panels

There are various technologies available, but the best solution for the often-cloudy British climate is to choose panels that use crystalline technology. These panels require only daylight to generate electricity, not bright, direct sunlight, so they will work even on overcast days.

The larger the panel you choose and the more you fit, the more electricity you will generate; a voltage regulator monitors the flow of electricity into a battery, where it is stored for use when required. The voltage regulator helps to prevent battery damage when you collect more energy than you actually need. Low-voltage appliances can be run direct from the battery, but most household appliances will require the installation of an inverter to transform the current to the conventional domestic rate for mains-voltage equipment.

Positioning the panels

The best position for the solar panels is on the sunniest, south-facing slope of a pitched roof, but even facing north a panel can work at up to 60 per cent of its maximum capacity. If you mount the panel on a flat roof, use brackets to lift it up at an angle, so that it will catch the sun's rays. It is possible to sell any surplus power that you generate back to the National Grid, but this is a complicated task and requires the installation of sophisticated 'grid synchronisation' equipment as well as establishing an unusual relationship with your energy provider. A better approach is to designate particular household appliances to use the power you produce, estimate how much energy you will need to collect and fit only the size and number of panels required to meet those needs.

WIRELESS LIGHT FOR OUTBUILDINGS

A simple solar-powered light circuit is a good option for a shed, summer house or other outbuilding that is not already connected to the power supply from the main house.

Kits are available for easy DIY installation and can produce enough power for up to seven hours of light, summer or winter. The panel is mounted on the shed roof and is connected to a battery pack situated inside. Cabling from the battery runs via a conventional switch to a lamp-holder and long-life, low-energy bulb mounted at a convenient place in the shed.

If you are fitting solar panels at the same time as renewing or building a roof, they can be incorporated into the main structure, in place of the normal roofing materials. Individual photovoltaic tiles are also available as a direct alternative to conventional roof tiles for all or part of a roof's area, but they are an expensive option. When fitting panels to an existing roof it is important to follow the manufacturer's instructions and allow the specified gap between the panels and the roof tiles beneath.

Assessing your power requirements

Solar panels are sold in watt ratings from 5W up to 150W and you can run as many as you have room for on your roof. Each panel is heavy, so seek the advice of the supplier, their professional fitters or a structural engineer before you make plans to mount a large number on a roof whose structure may not be strong enough to bear the weight.

How much energy do you need?
The energy consumption of household appliances and light bulbs is rated in watts. A 40W light bulb will draw 40W each hour from your battery, for example, so if it is switched on for 3 hours you will need a power supply of 120 watt hours. Consider how long an appliance or light is likely to be operating for each day and add up the total watt hours required.

What can the batteries store?
The capacity of the batteries fed by the PV panels is given in amp hours and each battery has a stated voltage, probably 12V. To calculate the watt hour capacity of your battery, multiply its amp hour rating by its

voltage. A 17 amp hour, 12 volt battery can store 204 (17 x 12) watt hours – enough to power a 204 watt appliance for one hour, a 102 watt appliance for two hours and so on.

How much power can the solar panels generate?

The third variable is the capacity of the solar panels you choose. To estimate how much power your panels will generate, multiply the panel's watt rating by the number of hours of sunshine it will be exposed to and then take away 15 per cent to allow for some natural wastage within the system. If you plan to use the electricity supplied from the panel all year round, it may be worth calculating your figures pessimistically, using a daylight hours rate based on winter conditions.

Once you know how much power you need to generate you can choose a system of panels and batteries with a capacity that can supply that, checking first that you have space on your roof for the panels and within the roof space or house for the necessary batteries.

Wind turbines

Since domestic wind turbines started appearing in large DIY stores, interest in home installations has increased dramatically. As with solar panels, the pay-back period for recouping your initial outlay in energy savings is many years, but they can still make a contribution, albeit small, to reducing your home's carbon dependence.

The most efficient systems are too large for use in most domestic situations – turbines can have a wingspan of 15m or more – but smaller rooftop options can generate up to 2.5kW of electricity and simply plug into the existing grid to augment your paid-for supply whenever wind power is available.

Permissions and planning

Before you consider purchasing a wind turbine, find out whether you will need to obtain planning permission to erect it. The planning laws relating to energy-saving devices have been relaxed to encourage greater use of them in homes, but there are still some size restrictions on the diameter of the blades and the height of the supporting post and planning permission is still required in some areas and on listed buildings.

You don't need to live on a blustery mountain, but the turbine will need sufficient wind on a regular basis to be

worth while, and the best way to maximise this is to mount the turbine high up. Ideally, a turbine should be 9m above any obstacle within 100m, but in an urban area this is almost certainly impossible to achieve. Turbines are heavy and the wind they need to operate can also make them unstable, so they need a firm base and strong fixings. Take advice from the manufacturer or supplier, or a structural engineer before you attempt to fit one to your house.

Where to put the turbine

In a built-up area, you are unlikely to be able to produce enough electricity to see large savings on your electricity bill. Turbines work best on fairly open ground, mounted on a free-standing mast away from buildings, which cause turbulence and interrupt the steady flow of air. The minimum average wind speed required over the course of a year is 6m/second. For rural areas, the British Wind Energy Association holds records of average wind speeds around the country, which can act as a useful guide. Alternatively, you could buy or hire an anemometer for several months to take your own wind-speed readings.

What else do you need?

Unlike solar panels, which can generate electricity in any weather as long as there is daylight, wind turbines will only turn when the wind speed exceeds a certain level. This means that the supply can be irregular and there may be days when no power is generated. If you plan to use your system only as and when power is available that need not matter, but if you hope to supply a dedicated circuit or appliance from your turbine, you will need to invest in batteries to store the power until it is needed.

Most batteries designed to accompany a wind microgeneration system can store three to four days' of electricity to make up for still days. An inverter is required to transform the power into the 240V supply needed by most domestic appliances.

Grants for improving your home's efficiency

The Government, local authorities and many energy providers run schemes offering grants to homeowners to encourage them to install loft or cavity wall insulation or to make other changes in and around the home to improve their property's energy efficiency.

The grants available to you will depend on your income, savings, age and whether you have children living with you, but some schemes are open to people in rented accommodation, as well as homeowners. Even the maximum grant is not always sufficient to fully cover the cost of the work, but you can make substantial savings on your energy bills that will quickly help you to recoup the initial outlay of the energy-saving measures you install.

Grants may be available to help you to replace the lightbulbs in your home with low-energy compact fluorescent tubes or to install cavity wall insulation or double-glazed windows.

Government grants

The Government's Warm Front scheme (known as Warm Homes in Northern Ireland, Warm Deal in Scotland and the Home Energy Efficiency Scheme in Wales) provides up to £2,700 in England (the maximum grant varies elsewhere) to householders claiming certain benefits in order to improve their heating and energy efficiency by installing better insulation or draughtproofing or by fitting thermostatic radiator valves or replacing their boiler.

The schemes are all means-tested and how much you can claim depends on your personal financial circumstances. Some scheme operators offer improvements free of charge; others are at a subsidised rate. You may also be able to purchase new, energy-efficient home appliances, such as washing machines or fridges, at a substantially reduced cost.

Grants from energy providers

As part of the Government's Energy Efficiency Commitment, all energy providers over a certain size are compelled to set and achieve targets for improved domestic energy efficiency. Your own energy provider will visit your home and carry out an energy survey, then suggest what improvements could be made and what grants are available to help, but in fact you are at liberty to contact any energy supply company, regardless of who provides you with your own gas or electricity.

Local council grants

All local authorities run schemes to help homeowners towards the cost of making energy-efficient home improvements. Contact your local council by telephone or writing to request relevant leaflets and information or search their website for details and online application forms that you can fill in.

HOW TO FIND OUT MORE

For impartial, free advice on saving energy, call the Energy Saving Trust efficiency helpline on 0845 727 7200 and you will be put through to a local office. Alternatively, visit their website at www.est.org.uk

For more information about grants that may be available to you, contact the following organisations:

Energy Efficiency Advice Centre
0800 512 012
www.saveenergy.org.uk

Age Concern
England: 0800 00 99 66
www.ageconcern.org.uk
Scotland: 0131 467 7118
www.ageconcernscotland.org.uk

Warm Front Hardship Fund
0800 408 0694
www.eage.co.uk

Making home improvements

The energy efficiency of new homes is tightly controlled and you will also have to satisfy stringent checks when altering or extending an existing property to be sure that its energy-efficiency is not compromised by the work you are doing.

Whenever you make even minor alterations to your home it is worth doing all you can to make sure that they improve your property's energy and water efficiency. If you are replacing plumbing fittings, look for new ones that use the minimum amount of water, such as slimline, dual-flush WCs or aerated taps and shower heads; if you are replacing guttering and downpipes, consider installing water butts or rainwater tanks at the same time; if you need to replace a rotten window, fit a double-glazed unit with the best insulation specifications you can.

If the work you are doing requires Building Regulations control and approval, the Building Control Officer will supervise the work to ensure that correct insulation is used throughout, that glass is of an adequate insulation level and that the work is of an acceptable standard.

Loft insulations

Home extensions and loft conversions are the most potentially contentious projects that you are likely to undertake. It is essential that in boarding a loft and turning it into a habitable room you do not compromise the level of insulation at the top of the house. Current Building Regulations specify a minimum of 270mm of loft insulation in a standard loft, but to prevent the room from being cold – and if it is open to a staircase from the storey below – you may decide to remove the existing insulation between the joists. It is essential that you insulate the roof slope to compensate before boarding it ready for decoration. You can do this with rigid insulation batts that can be cut to fit between the rafters (see page 49) or by spraying a special kind of foam insulation onto the underside of the roof, but this is a job for a professional.

Sun rooms and glass extensions

The impulse behind many home extensions is to create more light and space in an existing room and modern glass-roofed extensions are a popular and effective solution to the problem. While conservatories less than 30m^2 in area are exempt from Building Regulations Control, this only applies if the new structure is separated from the main house with doors. A walk-through, open-plan living or dining space will not fall into this category.

Glass is a poor insulator and a new structure that is largely constructed in this way is likely to seriously impact on the energy-efficiency of the house as a whole. Always choose the best specification of double glazing that you can, with at least a 24mm gap between the panes. Panels with the gap filled with argon are the most efficient. If the thickness of the two panes of glass differ this will also help to improve the panel's insulating properties.

Low-emissivity glass fitted as one of the panels in a double-glazed unit will go even further to improving their efficiency (see page 39). Look for Pilkington 'K' glass (see above) or an equivalent.

In the UK, the rate of heat loss is expressed in 'U values' and it is the overall U value of your home that must not be increased by the alterations you are making. The U value of windows are:

- Single clear glass   5.4
- Simple double glazing   2.6
- Double glazing with   1.8
  Low-emissivity glass
- Double glazing with   1.6
  Low-emissivity glass
  and argon

Installing a glazed extension of single-glazed clear glass will increase your home's U value dramatically, but even the best-quality low-E glass may not be insulating enough. However, if you can make improvements to the energy-losses elsewhere in the home you can offset this against the new extension to achieve the necessary permission. Consider increasing the level of insulation in the loft and adding cavity wall insulation wherever possible if it is not already installed. If the extension is being constructed as part of a larger renovation project, replacing old windows with modern double-glazed units will also make a big difference.

Planning permission for energy-saving improvements

It is currently necessary to seek planning permission for alterations that will change the outward appearance of your home. This includes wind turbines, solar panels and replacement windows, unless they are being fitted 'like-for-like'. If you are at all unsure whether your plans will require permission contact your local authority planning office for advice.

Insulation and ventilation

Insulation and ventilation

Insulation is vital when making your home energy efficient. Building Regulations stipulate the level of insulation required in various parts of the house. Ventilation is also needed for the healthy circulation of air.

Roof insulation

A modern house with a pitched roof and a loft used for storage should have insulation between (and possibly over) the ceiling joists, at least 200mm thick. On new builds, Building Regulations require 270mm. If the loft has been converted for use as a habitable room, the underside of the roof slope and the walls forming the loft room should be insulated to a similar standard. Flat roofs will incorporate insulation, probably as a warm roof structure.

If you have a pitched roof with less insulation than the current standards require, you can lay extra insulation over what is there already or you can insulate the roof slope (page 49). If you have a flat roof with inadequate insulation, consider converting it to a warm roof structure by adding insulation (see page 49).

Wall insulation

Modern homes incorporate insulation within their cavity walls to meet Building Regulations requirements. Timber-framed houses have insulation within their load-bearing wall panels. Older houses with unfilled cavity walls can be insulated by pumping insulation material into the cavity through holes drilled in the outer leaf of the wall. This is a job that must be carried out by an approved installer, and requires Building Regulations approval to ensure that the walls are in suitable condition and that the installation fills the cavity entirely.

Houses with solid walls have poor insulation performance, and improving this is a major undertaking. It can be done by insulating and dry-lining the external wall surfaces indoors using a series of battens and plasterboard.

External insulation is a less disruptive but more expensive option, which may need planning consent. It involves fixing insulation material to the wall surfaces and waterproofing it with timber or tile cladding, or with a layer of rendering applied over expanded metal mesh. It is a job for a specialist contractor.

Floor insulation

Houses with solid ground floors built since the early 1990s have to include a layer of insulation to meet Building Regulations requirements. Older houses have no such insulation, so ground floor slabs can feel very cold. Adding insulation involves laying rigid polystyrene boards over the existing floor surface and adding a new floating floor of chipboard – a process that raises the existing floor level by at least 70mm.

Suspended timber ground floors are easier to insulate, because insulation can be placed between the floor joists. However, the job will involve lifting and re-laying floorboards unless there is an accessible crawl space below the floor. Adding 100mm thick rigid insulation will improve the floor's insulation significantly.

Window and door insulation

Recently built and modernised houses will benefit from double-glazed windows, and efficiently draughtproofed door and window frames. In older houses, replacing existing single-glazed windows with double-glazed ones will significantly improve their insulation performance (pages 33–37). Replacing the glass in existing windows with double-glazed sealed units may be possible depending on the design of the frames, but may be as expensive as replacing the windows. Installing secondary glazing inside the existing windows will be cheaper but is not as effective.

If existing doors and windows are not draughtproofed, installing the relevant products is a simple job to tackle on a DIY basis (pages 38–44).

Ventilation

Appropriate ventilation is essential in four main areas of the home.
• Lofts must be ventilated to prevent condensation within the roof space.
• Voids beneath suspended timber ground floors need ventilation to prevent rot.
• Kitchens and bathrooms need ventilation to disperse cooking odours and steam. Extractor fans are useful for this.
• Adequate ventilation is mandatory in rooms containing fuel-burning appliances such as boilers and gas fires.

Choosing double glazing

Double glazing – having two layers of glass instead of one in a window – traps a layer of still air or inert gas between the panes. This acts as an insulator, but the warm inner pane also reduces cold down-draughts from the window and prevents condensation. Although double glazing will not save much on fuel bills, it will greatly increase indoor comfort. There are two main types: single sealed units and secondary double glazing.

Sealed units Two panes of glass separated by a spacer are bonded together and sealed at the factory before being fitted into the window frame. The panes may be separated by between 6mm and 24mm; wide gaps give better insulation than narrow ones.

Secondary double glazing A pane of glass or plastic is fixed to the window frame, leaving an air gap between it and the existing glass. This is less effective than a sealed unit unless the opening part of the window is well draught-proofed. Condensation in the gap can be a problem in cold weather.

Triple glazing A wide air gap between panes of glass (100–200mm) insulates effectively against noise, but is too wide to retain heat. Triple glazing combines a sealed twin-pane unit with a third pane, like secondary glazing, to provide excellent heat and sound insulation.

Replacement windows

Many householders acquire double glazing when having old windows replaced. All double-glazing companies offer windows (usually made from uPVC – unplasticised polyvinyl chloride – with steel internal reinforcement) that are fitted with tailor-made sealed units.

Since April 2002, all window and door installations have had to be carried out by a FENSA (Fenestration Self-Assessment) registered company. The contractor should give you a certificate to show that the double-glazing units comply with the latest Building Regulations. In particular, the regulations state that any uPVC windows must have a thermal insulation U-value of $2.0W/(m^2.K)$ and aluminium windows $2.2W/(m^2.K)$.

HOW DOUBLE GLAZING WORKS

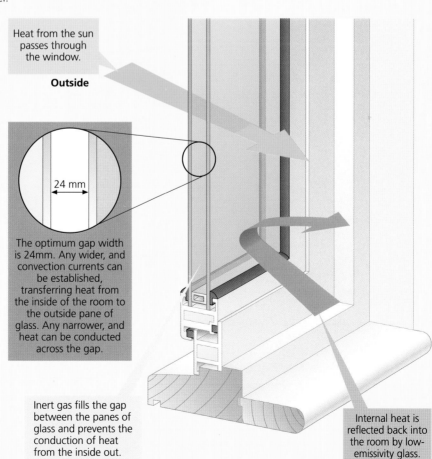

Heat from the sun passes through the window.

Outside

24 mm

The optimum gap width is 24mm. Any wider, and convection currents can be established, transferring heat from the inside of the room to the outside pane of glass. Any narrower, and heat can be conducted across the gap.

Inert gas fills the gap between the panes of glass and prevents the conduction of heat from the inside out.

Internal heat is reflected back into the room by low-emissivity glass.

Replacing double-glazed panes

Cracked or failed double-glazed units that are letting in condensation should be replaced promptly to maintain their efficiency. The method depends on the type of unit.

Before you start Double-glazing units must be bought ready-made to the size of your window from a glass merchant or double-glazing supplier.

Sealed stepped units

Replacing sealed stepped double glazing is similar to fitting a single sheet of glass, except that spacer blocks are fitted in the rebate of the window to keep the stepped part of the double-glazed unit clear of the frame.

Retain the old spacer blocks so they can be re-used, or buy new ones from your glass merchant. Window companies are unlikely to sell them.

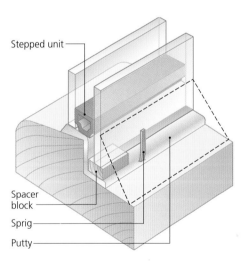

Stepped unit

Spacer block

Sprig

Putty

1 Place the spacer blocks in a bed of putty about 300mm apart along the bottom of the rebate.

2 Stand the double-glazed pane on the blocks and fix it in place with sprigs all round. Apply putty to the outside of the window in the normal way.

Square-edge units

Glazing beads are usually screwed into the outside of the window to hold square-edged double-glazing units in place.

1 Unscrew the glazing beads before removing the broken glass.

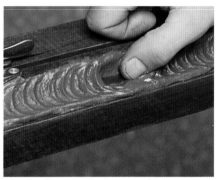

2 Put a bed of non-setting putty (available from glass merchants) around the rebate. Press spacer blocks into the putty (two blocks spaced well apart on each of the four sides).

3 Lift the sealed unit into place on the spacers and press it well back into the rebate.

4 Coat the glazing beads with non-setting putty on the inside face and press them tightly in place against the glazing units.

5 Fix the beads in place with brass screws.

Aluminium or plastic windows

The glass is often in rubber gaskets, making replacement difficult. Call in a glazier or ask the manufacturer for details on glass replacement for your particular model of window.

Four secondary double-glazing systems

A house can be fitted with secondary double glazing relatively cheaply using materials that give effective results. It must be removed in summer and may not look attractive, nevertheless the cost saving compared with having replacement windows is considerable.

Study the fitting instructions supplied with the system you choose and follow them carefully. Double check your measurements before you order glass or rigid plastic sheet. Mistakes can be expensive.

Clean the windows, inside and out, before you start work. If you are using a system that involves adhesive tape, make sure the window frame is clean and dry. The tape will not stick to surfaces that are dirty or damp.

Existing window glass   Secondary glazing fixed to internal window frame

How secondary double glazing works
Secondary double-glazing systems are fitted on the inside of an existing window. The secondary panel is usually fixed to the inside of the frame, creating a gap the depth of the frame between the exterior glass and the double glazing. Hinged or sliding systems are available from glazing companies or in kit form, allowing you to open the window without removing the double glazing.

Insulating film

A clear plastic film is stuck to the window frame and then shrunk with gentle heat from a hair dryer to remove wrinkles. Although this is not a permanent system, you could extend its life by attaching the plastic film to a frame of timber battens. The framework could be taken down when not required and kept for later use.

Tools *Scissors; hair dryer.*

Materials *Kit containing clear film and double-sided adhesive tape.*

1 Cut a sheet of film a little larger than the window, so that it overlaps all round the window frame by about 50mm.

2 Stick the double-sided adhesive tape around the frame.

3 Remove the backing from the tape and press the film against it, working from the top downwards and keeping it as taut as possible.

4 Warm the film with a hair dryer to remove wrinkles. Finally, trim off the excess film with the scissors.

Plastic channelling

Strips of plastic channelling are fitted along the edges of a sheet of glass or rigid plastic. They are then fixed to the window frame with screws and fixing clips.

Some systems have hinged channelling that allows the secondary glazing to be opened. Other types are fixed to the window frame all round and cannot be opened. They have to be taken down completely in summer before any windows can be opened.

Measure the window to allow for the glass or rigid plastic to overlap onto the frame, leaving enough space for the fixing clips to be screwed to the frame.

Tools *Trimming knife or tenon saw (depending on the type of channelling); pencil; bradawl; screwdriver. Perhaps a mitre box.*

Materials *Sheet of 4mm glass or 2–4mm rigid plastic; plastic channelling; screws; fixing clips.*

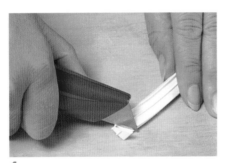

1 Cut the channelling to fit the four edges of the glass or plastic sheet. Mitre the ends to give a neat fit. If the channelling is rigid you will need a tenon saw or hacksaw and a mitre box. Push the channelling onto the glass or plastic sheet.

2 Hold the framed pane over the window while a helper marks positions for the fixing holes, following the maker's instructions for spacing.

3 Deepen the marked spots with the bradawl to provide pilot holes, and screw the fixing clips and glazing in place.

Fixing with Velcro tape

Rigid plastic sheet can be fixed with self-adhesive touch-and-close fastening tape, such as Velcro.
• When you are buying the plastic, measure it to overlap 15mm on all sides of the window frame.
• Do not use glass, because it is too heavy for the system.
• The double glazing can be removed when necessary but the loop part of the tape will have to remain in place and it may look unsightly and collect dirt.

Tools *Scissors.*

Materials *Self-adhesive touch-and-close fastening tape; 2–4mm thick clear rigid plastic; foam-strip draught excluder.*

1 Cut several pieces of tape about 40mm long. It is too expensive to use in long strips.

2 Peel the backing paper off the loop (soft) side of the tape and fix it in place at intervals around the window frame.

EMERGENCY COVER

A cracked window is not only a potential danger but will allow cold air into the house and warm air out. Seal a cracked pane temporarily with transparent waterproof glazing tape, applied to the outside. If the pane is smashed, cover the whole window with heavy gauge polythene secured by timber battens nailed around the frame from the outside.

3 Leave the backing paper on the hook side of the tape, and press the pieces onto the loop strips.

4 Stick foam-strip draught excluder between the patches to prevent draughts.

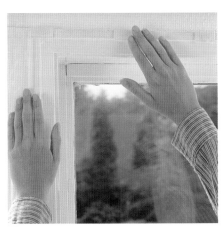

5 Peel off the remaining backing paper from the tape and press the pane in place.

Magnetic fixing tape

Rigid plastic sheets can be fitted as secondary glazing using magnetic fixing strip. The strip has two self-adhesive parts, a magnetic strip that adheres to the plastic and a metal strip to go on the frame.
• The system is designed for use with plastic up to 4mm thick. Never use it with glass because it is not strong enough to hold the weight.
• Have the plastic cut slightly larger than the window so that it overlaps onto the frame by about 25mm.

Tools *Scissors or trimming knife.*

Materials *Magnetic fixing strip; 2–4mm thick clear rigid plastic.*

1 Cut the strip to fit around the plastic, mitring the corners with sharp scissors or a trimming knife.

2 Stick the strip to the plastic, with the metal half upwards.

3 Press the sheet to the frame. The metal strip will stay on the frame when the plastic pane is removed.

4 The metal strip can be covered with a thin coat of paint to match the window frame. This makes it less noticeable when the sheet is removed. When redecorating, rub the surface with fine abrasive paper to prevent a build-up of paint.

Draughtproofing a window

Draughtproofing your windows is a simple and effective way of reducing heat loss and therefore improving the energy efficiency of your home.

Before you start Clean the window frame with water and a little washing-up liquid to remove all grease and dirt. Rinse and wait for the surface to dry.

A casement window

Most of the draughtproofing strips on the market (page 42) are suitable for use on a wooden casement window. Only the strips with an adhesive backing can be used on a metal casement window.

1 Cut lengths to fit with scissors or a trimming knife.

2 Peel away the protective backing as you stick down each length on the rebate. Make sure that one piece of excluder goes right into each corner.

Silicone sealant for large gaps For large or uneven gaps, a silicone sealant (also called a frame sealant) is particularly useful. It can also be used on doors, but not on sash windows. Read any advice on the container before you begin (page 39).

A sash window

Rigid brush strip is the most suitable material for sealing the sides of a sash window, as the sashes slide over it easily.

1 Measure the height of the sliding sashes and cut four pieces of brush strip – two pieces for each sash.

2 Fix the strip to either side of the frame – on the inside of the inner sash and on the outside of the outer sash. Use pre-holed strip, fixing it with the pins provided and a hammer. Unless the window remains closed for most of the time, self-adhesive strip is not suitable because it is unlikely to withstand the friction from the sashes as they slide. Replace the sashes and beading.

3 Seal the gap at the top and bottom of the sashes with any of the more durable foam strips, which should be fixed to the frame or the sash.

4 If there is a draught between the top and bottom sashes of the window, fix nylon brush pile strip to the bottom sash at the meeting point.

LOW-EMISSIVITY GLASS

As part of the Government's Energy Efficiency Initiative, the Glass and Glazing Federation (GGF) and the Energy Saving Trust have been working together to promote to homeowners the benefits of double glazing. They are also trying to raise awareness of low emissivity – or Low-E – glass, which saves even more energy.

Low-E glass has a microscopically thin coating on one side. This high-quality glass forms the inner pane of a double-glazing unit, with the coating facing the cavity. The coating reflects heat from the room surfaces back into the building, but it also allows solar energy to pass through into the house.

The coating is virtually invisible, although the window may look as if it is covered in a transparent film in certain strong, oblique lighting.

The GGF suggests that Low-E glass is as energy efficient as triple glazing, without the 50 per cent increase in weight and the extra thickness that is involved.

Energy saving is improved still further if the gap between the panes in a double-glazed unit is filled with an inert gas, such as argon, rather than air, as it has better thermal insulation properties.

Gaps around a window frame

Gaps around the outside of the window frames – as well as poorly maintained paintwork – will allow water to get in resulting in damp appearing on the internal walls around the window. It will also encourage rot to attack the frames.

Using frame sealant

Cracks up to about 10mm wide in your window frames can be filled with frame sealant (see panel, page 40).

Tools *Trimming knife; thin screwdriver; clean rag.*

Materials *Frame sealant and applicator. Perhaps a jar of water.*

1 With a trimming knife, cut the nozzle off the sealant cartridge at an angle to give the necessary width of sealant to fill the gap. Break the foil seal or cut the sealed top of the cartridge.

2 Wipe around the frame with a clean rag, and inject a bead of sealant into the crack all round. The sealant should be placed in the angle between the window frame and the wall.

For neatness, try to inject the sealant in a single run without stopping, except at corners. Release the trigger to stop the flow.

3 If it is necessary to smooth the sealant, use a wet finger.

4 Sealant can be painted once a skin has formed (one to three weeks), but it is not necessary to do so.

CHOOSING FRAME SEALANT

Frame sealant is commonly available from hardware shops and DIY stores in three colours – white, brown and transparent, but other colours are sometimes available.

The sealant is sold in a cartridge that may either have a screw-down applicator or has to be fitted into a trigger-operated sealant gun. The gun is not expensive to buy and will last indefinitely.

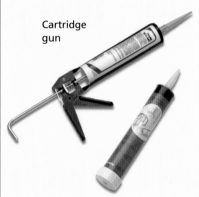

Cartridge gun

Screw-down applicator

Expanding foam filler

For large, irregular gaps that are hard to reach, use a can of expanding foam filler. This adheres to most building materials. It is injected by nozzle at any angle, after which it expands in volume, effectively sealing even hidden areas. Once hardened, the foam is heat, cold and water resistant and rot-proof. It can be cut, sanded, plastered or painted.

HELPFUL TIP

If you cannot find the source of a draught, light a candle and hold it in front of the door or window. Move around the edge of the frame and the flame will flicker at the point where the draught is coming in. Take care not to set curtains alight.

Sealing with mortar

If the gap is more than about 10mm wide it should be filled with mortar, which is available in small bags – ideal for jobs of this scale.

Tools *Plant sprayer; small trowel or filling knife; trimming knife; clean rag.*

Materials *Water; mortar; sealant and applicator.*

1 Dampen the crack with water. A plant sprayer is ideal.

2 Press the mortar in place with a small trowel or filling knife, so that it is level with the surface of the brickwork.

3 When the mortar has hardened, which will take two or three days, seal all round the frame with frame sealant (see page 39).

Draughtproofing a door

Draughts are uncomfortable and a sign of a poorly insulated house. To ensure your doors are a snug fit, you may need to use more than one type of draught excluder – a foam strip around the sides and top, and a threshold excluder at the bottom.

If you are fitting a foam, rubber or flexible strip for the first time – or are unsure which excluder is most suitable – experiment on one door before you buy all the material you need. To calculate how much of a strip draught excluder you need to buy, measure the height and width of the door.

Some threshold excluders are designed to deflect in-blown rain as well as to stop draughts. Threshold excluders are usually sold in standard lengths for external doors and some come in two parts – one to fix to the base of the door and the other part to fix to the sill.

Adding an enclosed porch

If you put an enclosed porch around an outside door – especially if it is exposed to prevailing winds – you will greatly reduce the draughts. You will also help to reduce condensation inside the house if you can leave wet umbrellas and coats in a porch.

There are regulations that govern extending in front of the house building line, but porches are exempt from planning permission providing the floor area is not more than 3m² and no part is higher than 3m above ground level. You must ensure that the porch is at least 2m from the boundary between the garden and a road or public footpath. Porches are also exempt from Building Regulations control if the total floor area is under 3m².

HELPFUL TIP

To improve the adhesion of self-adhesive strips, apply a thin coating of clear, all-purpose adhesive over the surface to which the excluder is to be fixed. Let the glue dry before pressing on the strips.

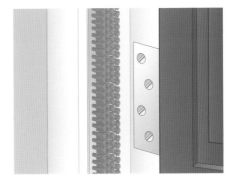

Strip excluders for the frame
Self-adhesive foam strips or nylon brush strip are cut to length and fitted to the frame. Some require pinning.

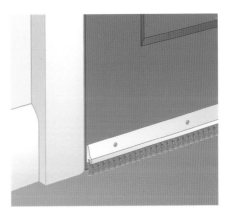

Strip excluders for the base of the door
A strip of nylon, rubber or plastic bristle mounted in aluminium. The excluder is fitted to the base of the door – on the inside – and is usually adjustable for height to give a good seal.

Letterbox excluder A plastic frame with two rows of nylon bristles fits over the inside of a letterbox.

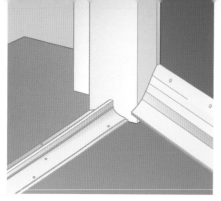

Two-piece excluders fitted to door and sill
A weatherbar is attached to the sill and a deflector is attached to the base of the door. The deflector is shaped to deflect rainwater over the weatherbar when the door is closed and the weatherbar prevents rain from being blown in beneath the door.

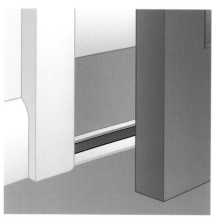

Metal or rubber seal for the sill
A plastic or metal bar fitted to the sill has a rubber insert that seals the gap under the door when it is closed.

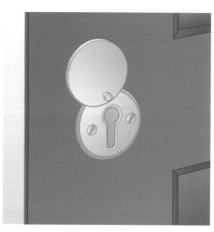

Keyhole cover A pivoted cover, or escutcheon, hangs in front of the keyhole of a mortise lock.

Choosing a draught excluder

Before you buy a draught excluder, measure the width of the gaps that need to be blocked. The packaging on most draught excluders indicates how big a gap the product is intended to fill and where it can be used.

Self-adhesive foam strip
Use on casement windows and exterior doors. Quality varies a lot. Some strips perish after only one or two seasons; more expensive types will last for five years or more. Cheaper versions are made of polyurethane, which hardens with age. Sizes vary according to the manufacturer but strips are usually about 6mm thick and 10mm wide. Most strips are only supplied in white. Avoid getting paint on foam – it will harden with age, unless the strip manufacturer states otherwise.

Self-adhesive rubber strip
Use on casement windows and exterior doors. Available in a limited colour range and in profiles including P and E. This type of excluder is tough and will last longer than foam. Fix to the frame as for self-adhesive foam strip (above).

Brush strips
Use on exterior and patio doors, and on sash and casement windows. The strips consist of siliconised nylon pile in self-adhesive strips or in a metal plastic holder that is to be tacked to the frame, not the door or window. The strip is particularly designed for surfaces that move against each other, as on sash windows and patio doors.

Draughtproofing a timber ground floor

Air can come up into the room if the boards are merely butted together, particularly in older properties, making it cold and increasing your energy consumption.

Draughtproofing a floor depends on the size of the gaps. Fill large gaps (wider than 6mm) with wood. Smaller gaps can be filled with mastic applied via a sealant gun. The mastic colour does not matter if you are laying a new floor covering. If you intend to sand the boards, choose a sealant close to the desired colour, or one that will absorb stain when you apply it to the boards. Rot will not set in after you have sealed the gaps as long as air can move freely beneath the floor through airbricks.

Large gaps

Tools *Mallet; plane; power sander or flap-wheel attachment on a power drill.*

Materials *Thin strips of softwood planed to a wedge section; PVA wood adhesive.*

1 Apply adhesive to the two long sides of a wedged strip of wood.

2 Tap the wood into place with a mallet (below), aiming to make its top edge flush with the floor surface.

3 When the adhesive has set, use a power sander or a flap-wheel power drill attachment (above) to smooth any raised parts of the strip.

WHEN THE FLOOR IS TO BE COVERED

If you are laying a floor covering, you do not need to fill the gaps between the floorboards. Instead, lay sheets of hardboard over the whole floor. This will provide a flat surface for the new floor covering as well as draughtproofing the floor. If the cracks are small and the floorboards are level, lay foil-coated building paper – foil side up – under a carpet. This is cheaper than hardboard, and will stop draughts and also reflect some warmth back into the room.

Small gaps

Tools *Sealant gun; filling knife for removing excess.*

Materials *Flooring sealant cartridges; lining paper or similar for wiping excess filler from knife (newspaper will cause black stains).*

1 Check the width of the largest gap between the boards, and cut the cartridge nozzle off at an angle to give a bead of the correct width.

2 Load the cartridge into the sealant gun and squeeze the trigger to start the flow of filler.

3 Draw the nozzle along each joint in turn, allowing the filler to sink in.

4 As you complete each joint, use the filling knife to remove excess filler and wipe the blade on some lining paper or similar material. Repeat the process to fill each joint in turn.

SEALING THE GAP BELOW A SKIRTING BOARD

A skirting board is often fitted so there is a gap between it and the floor. If carpet has not been pushed into this gap, draughts may come up from below a timber floor.

To seal a gap, use panel pins to fix quadrant beading (see picture) to the base of the skirting board, pressing it tight to the floor. Do not pin the beading to the floor, because this will prevent the boards from expanding and contracting, as they normally do when the weather varies from damp to dry.

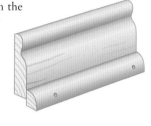

INSULATING TIMBER FLOORS

If you are having work done and all the floorboards in a downstairs room have to be lifted, take the opportunity to fit underfloor insulation.

One way is to staple nylon garden netting across the joists and place lengths of loft insulation blanket between them. Draw the netting up tight so the blanket does not sag between the joists.

The other way is to cut rigid foam insulation boards into strips to match the joist spacing and support them on battens nailed to the joist sides.

Insulating your home

Approximately half of the heat lost from an average home disappears through the walls and loft. To improve energy efficiency and cut utility bills, check to see whether your home is properly insulated.

By insulating your cavity walls and loft, you can reduce your fuel bills significantly – and easily. If your home has not been insulated, 26 per cent of the heat lost will disappear through the roof. Look at the roofs of the houses in your street next time there is a covering of snow. Well-insulated houses will retain their heat inside and the snow will stay on the roof for longer through the day. On poorly insulated houses the escaping heat will quickly melt the snow.

Not only will loft insulation save you, typically, around £200 a year, it will also benefit the environment by reducing carbon emissions by around one and a half tonnes over the same period.

Pages 46–49 show you, step-by-step, how you can install loft or roof insulation yourself. An alternative method is to use spray-on insulation: a foam product that is sprayed onto the inside of the roof slope and sets to a hard material, which is an excellent insulator. This is a job for the professionals, but a very effective solution and sometimes the only option in older buildings. It not only insulates against heat loss through the roof covering, but it also seals gaps between slates or tiles, creating a weather-proof barrier.

A further 10 per cent of heat loss escapes via gaps around uninsulated doors and floors. By eliminating gaps in your floors and below skirting boards you will save a further £10–£20 and reduce carbon dioxide emissions by a further 120kg over the year.

Grants and offers available

Insulating your home need not be expensive. If you are considering making improvements there are a range of grants and offers available.

One example is the HEAT project, which was set up in 1997 by Enact Energy and is now endorsed by over 100 local authorities across England and Wales. Funded via the EEC, to date it has helped more than 300,000 households to insulate their homes.

Before starting work on your home, check first to see if you are eligible for assistance. See page 27 for more information about what is available and how to find out more.

Insulating a loft

A poorly insulated loft is the biggest cause of heat loss from a home. Even if you already have some insulation between the joists, by topping it up to the recommended depth of 270mm, additional heat will be retained.

If you put down flooring-grade chipboard after you have insulated between the joists, you will have a useful storage area. But remember the joists are only ceiling joists for the room below, not floor joists, so you cannot use the space as a room or store too many heavy things there.

Before you start Clear the floor space and vacuum the loft. At the same time, check for woodworm and rot, and, if necessary, call in a specialist contractor to treat it.

If the loft has no lighting, run a table lamp or inspection lamp off an extension cable from a socket downstairs. A torch will not give adequate light for the job.

Fixing a vapour barrier on the floor

Tools *Scissors.*

Materials *Rolls of reflective foil building paper or sheets of polythene; masking tape.*

1 Cut the material with scissors so that it is about 50–75mm wider than the gap between the joists.

2 Lay the material in the gap. Remember that reflective foil paper must be laid foil-side down.

3 Seal any overlaps in the material with 50mm masking tape.

Laying an insulation blanket on the floor

The spacing between joists varies but about 350mm is average. Do not cut the excess off a 400mm blanket – let it curl up on each side to make a snug fit.

Tools *Scissors; face mask; protective gloves.*

Materials *Rolls of glass fibre or mineral wool blanket.*

1 Start unrolling the blanket between two joists at the eaves at one end of the loft.

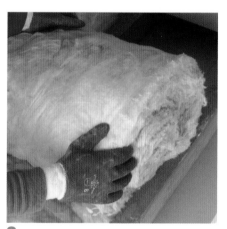

2 Do not take the material right into the eaves; you must leave a gap of about 50mm so that air can come in through the soffit and flow through the loft. If the air cannot circulate, condensation may form.

3 Press the blanket down lightly as you unroll it so that it lies flat but do not squash it so that it becomes compressed.

PROTECTING YOURSELF

Insulating products can be extremely irritating. Open the packaging in the loft and keep the hatch closed while you are working. Wear protective gloves and overalls or a long-sleeved shirt, and tuck sleeves and trouser legs into gloves and socks. If fibres do get into the gloves, they will cause more irritation than if you wore no gloves at all. Wear a face mask and throw it away after use. Wear a safety helmet to protect your head against the rafters.

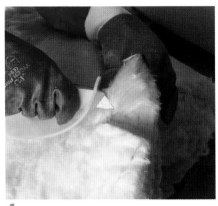

4 When you reach the other side of the loft, cut the blanket with scissors or a knife. Special guards are available to fit to your knife; they both compress the insulation blanket while you cut and help to protect your hands. Again, take care not to block the ventilation gaps under the eaves.

5 Continue to lay insulation between the other joists. When joining two rolls, make a butt join, pressing the ends close to each other. Cut the insulation so that it fits tightly around pipes.

6 Try to slip insulation under loose electric cables to prevent them overheating. Where practicable, fix cables to the sides of the joists to keep them out of the way.

7 Never insulate under the cold water cistern. Leave a gap in the insulation so that warm air from below will keep the chill off the base of the cistern and help to prevent the water from freezing.

Insulating with loose-fill

Pour loose-fill granules between the joists and level out. Make a levelling gauge so that the granules are at an even depth. Most ceiling joists are 100–150mm deep so filling level with the top will not provide adequate insulation. The joists must be made deeper by nailing 50mm square battens to the top. Do not spread insulation on top of the joists as you cannot see where it is safe to walk.
Cut a piece of scrap wood to a wide T-shape that will fit the gap above the loose-fill. The 'arms' should rest on top of the joists, so that when you run the gauge between two joists the granules are spread to a consistent depth.

THE IMPORTANCE OF VENTILATION

A good flow of air across the loft is important for keeping the roof timbers dry. In old lofts without roofing felt under the tiles or slates, air blows in and out through the gaps. If the roof has a layer of felt under the battens, then this prevents air coming in. Some modern roofs have ventilation around the eaves and also often at high level. Any insulation laid under the felt on the underside of the roof slope must allow ventilation to continue in order to clear any moisture from the surface of the felt. A gap of 50mm behind the insulation is usually enough to ensure good ventilation, provided there is room at the ridge for the air to escape and room at the eaves for it to enter.

HELPFUL TIP

When laying an insulation blanket, use a broom to push the blanket into the areas that are hard to reach.

LAGGING A LOFT-HATCH DOOR

• Cut a piece of glass-fibre or mineral-fibre blanket or thick, expanded polystyrene sheet to fit above the loft hatch.
• To fix the blanket, hammer two or three nails along each edge of the door. Tie string over the material and loop it around the nails to hold it in place. Do not pull the string so tight that it squashes the blanket.
• Alternatively, cut a piece of polythene sheet large enough to cover the blanket. Fix the sheet over the blanket, holding the edges in place with drawing pins.
• If you are using polystyrene sheet, stick it to the door with polystyrene ceiling tile adhesive.
• Make sure that the hatch door is a tight fit. Fix a draught excluder (page 41) to the rebate so that damp air cannot pass through into the cold loft above and possibly cause condensation problems.

Choosing loft insulation

You can insulate a loft yourself with blanket, loose-fill or sheet insulation. Alternatively, pay a specialist company to blow loose-fill insulation between the joists. Lay at least 270mm of insulation: the minimum recommended in the current Building Regulations. A thicker layer will prevent even more heat loss. You may be eligible for a grant – ask your local council or Citizens Advice Bureau for details.

How much material do I need?
Measure the length and width of your house and then multiply the two figures to calculate the area of the loft floor. Most insulation states the area the packet will cover. Some suppliers will deliver – blanket rolls are bulky and transporting enough to insulate a whole loft is likely to require a van.

Blanket rolls
Mineral wool or glass-fibre blanket is supplied in rolls 100–200mm thick. Standard rolls are 400mm wide; combi-rolls are 1200mm wide and have guidelines so the roll can be cut into two 600mm or three 400mm wide pieces.

Foil backed blankets are also available and provide the insulating properties of a standard layer of mineral wool blanket in a thickness of only around 10mm. They are expensive, but a useful option for topping up existing insulation without losing head-height in the loft.
- Use a panel saw to cut through the roll while it is still in its wrapper, or you can cut through single widths with sharp scissors.

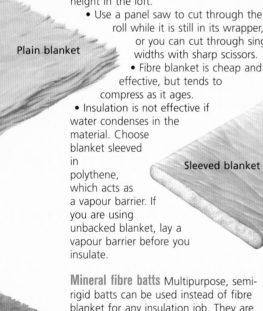

Plain blanket

- Fibre blanket is cheap and effective, but tends to compress as it ages.
- Insulation is not effective if water condenses in the material. Choose blanket sleeved in polythene, which acts as a vapour barrier. If you are using unbacked blanket, lay a vapour barrier before you insulate.

Sleeved blanket

Mineral fibre batts
Multipurpose, semi-rigid batts can be used instead of fibre blanket for any insulation job. They are available in thicknesses from 25mm to 100mm, so two or more batts will be needed to meet the minimum depth required for insulating a floor. Batts are 1200mm long and 600mm or 900mm wide, which makes them less bulky and easier to handle than blanket rolls – but they are more costly.

Loose-fill

This is supplied in sacks, each one sufficient to insulate 1m² of loft space. The loose-fill is simply poured between the joists. The depth of the joist may need to be increased so that the required depth of 270mm of cover is achieved.
- Common loose-fill materials are vermiculite granules or mineral fibre. Granules can also be used to top up old blanket insulation.
- Granules will blow about in a draughty loft, so pin building paper to the joists over the granules. Leave the tops of the joists visible so you can walk safely.
- Allow for joists when estimating quantities – or there will be too much left over.

Expanded polystyrene sheets
Useful for sliding into areas that have been boarded over or are difficult to reach – the flat roof over an extension, for example. It can also be used to insulate a cold water cistern but is too expensive to use to insulate your entire loft.
- Expanded polystyrene is available as squeeze-fit 60mm thick slabs 610 x 402mm and as 50mm thick general purpose 1200 x 450mm sheets. Specialist outlets will also cut polystyrene to your exact requirements. Make sure it is fire retardant. Type A FRA will conform to BS4735 for combustibility.

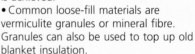

Reflective foil building paper
Acts as a vapour barrier so that moisture cannot condense in the insulation material. Heat also reflects off the shiny surface – either back into the house in winter or back into the loft in summer.
- Lay the foil between joists or drape it over them. If using it between joists to stop loose granules blowing about, pin the paper in position. There is no need to pin it if it is laid on the floor beneath insulation.
- It is supplied in 25m or 50m rolls 900mm wide by builders' merchants.

Insulating a roof

If you want to use your loft for storing items that need to be kept warm and dry it is advisable to insulate the underside of the roof, rather than the loft floor.

Tools *Knife or large pair of scissors; staple gun. Possibly power drill.*

Materials *Glass-fibre insulation batts; garden netting. Building paper, hardboard sheets or foil-faced plasterboard; drywall screws.*

1 Hold a length of insulation up to the underside of the roof and mark the width of the rafter gaps on the insulation.

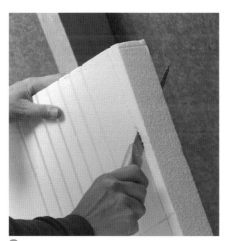

2 Using scissors or knife, cut the insulation to fit between the rafters. Small off-cuts can be placed in the eaves first, to provide a spacing to maintain the air gap.

3 Do not hammer anything into the rafter because you could dislodge a tile or slate. Use a staple gun and nylon garden netting to hold the insulation in place. You may need a helper for this part of the task.

4 For a quick, simple finish, staple sheets of building paper to the rafters. Where two strips of building paper join, make sure they overlap by at least 100mm and tape along the join with waterproof adhesive tape. Alternatively, screw hardboard sheets to the rafters.

5 For an even better finish, you can screw foil-faced plasterboard to the rafters, as shown. The foil should face the roof. Use plasterboard drywall screws, which can be put in with a power drill.

Options for a flat roof

Flat roofs should be insulated at the time they are built. If you are having a flat-roofed extension added to your house, make sure that insulation is incorporated when the roof is constructed.

Flat roofs must be ventilated above the insulation to prevent condensation on the timbers. You can do this by drilling small holes in the fascia or soffit board to take ventilator insect screens.

• If an existing roof lacks insulation, remove a fascia board so that you can see into the space between the roof lining and ceiling. The fascia board will either be nailed or screwed to the ends of the ceiling joists.

• Slide sheets of expanded polystyrene – 75mm thick – into the gap. If you cannot take off a fascia board, line the ceiling below, preferably with thermal board.

• You can place insulation above the roof decking if access to the roof void is not possible. The simplest method involves laying sheets of rigid polystyrene or other expanded foam insulation on the roof decking, covering it with a permeable geotextile membrane and placing a layer of ballast on top to keep it in place.

Insulating the walls of a house

Cavity walls

Insulating cavity walls saves heat loss from a house, but it is not a DIY job. To check if the cavities have already been filled, you can drill a hole into the cavity from the outside and feel with a probe. If it is empty, call in a contractor specialising in cavity insulation.

As it is impossible to check how well the work has been done or how long it will last, you will have to rely on the contractor's integrity. You can get advice from the National Insulation Association, 2 Vimy Court, Vimy Road, Leighton Buzzard LU7 1FG; tel 01525 383313; www.nationalinsulationassociation.org.uk

Walls to be insulated must show no sign of penetrating damp. The cause of any damp must be cured first and the walls allowed to dry out. The contractor should examine the walls thoroughly to make sure they are fit for filling, with no evidence of damp, or damage that may let in damp.

There are two main insulation systems to choose between, with similar installation methods.

Mineral-wool fibres or polystyrene beads

The dry system consists of mineral-wool fibres or expanded polystyrene beads being blown through holes drilled in the outer leaf of the wall until the cavity is filled.

Expanding foam

With the second system, the cavities are filled with foam. This is produced on site and pumped through holes drilled in the outer brick leaf. The foam normally dries after a few days and becomes firm. This is not suitable for timber-framed houses.

Solid walls

Any extra width of insulation on the inside of a wall may bring the wall out beyond skirting boards, picture rails and architraves. Often lights, wall sockets, light switches and radiators will have to be repositioned.

Insulate the walls with thermal board fixed to battens. Before nailing the boards in place, pin fibre blanket to the battens.

Alternatively, fix the thermal board direct to the walls with the adhesive suggested by the board manufacturer, and a secondary fixing of hammer-in fixings or screws.

Dry-lining a wall with plasterboard

Dry lining is a good way of insulating a solid wall. An air gap created between the wall and the new boards helps to reduce heat loss and can be filled with insulation.

Thermal board, which has a polystyrene backing for insulation, can be fixed direct to a plastered wall provided the wall is flat. It is held with a special adhesive and hammer-in fixings. If the wall is not flat, a timber framework is needed to provide a level surface.

How many boards do I need?

The boards do not have to fit the height of the wall exactly – a gap of up to 25mm is usually left at the bottom for expansion, and may be covered by the skirting board. Boards need not be fitted vertically. They can be fitted horizontally if this is more convenient for the wall measurements.

1 Measure the height of the wall at each end (the heights may be slightly different, so use the highest figure). Also measure the width at the top and bottom.

2 From these measurements work out how many boards you need. If the widths will not fit exactly, plan to place the boards so that narrow widths will fit equally at each end of the wall.

3 Allow for separate pieces of board above door frames and above and below windows.

4 If the wall height is considerably more than the board length, fit the boards in staggered long and short upper and lower panels. Or fix the boards horizontally.

Fixing battens to the walls

Remove wall fittings, such as picture rails and skirting boards, carefully so they can be replaced later. All switches and sockets will have to be moved forward. Take down architraves and refit them on the lining.

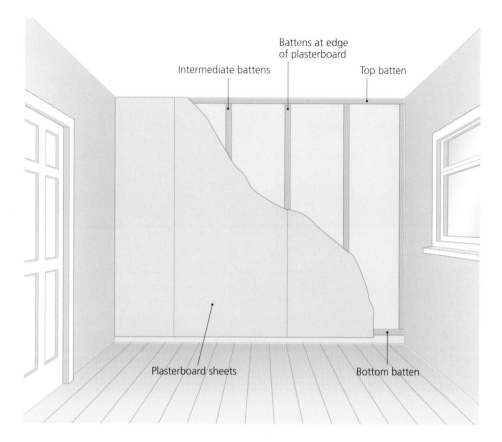

Intermediate battens

Battens at edge of plasterboard

Top batten

Plasterboard sheets

Bottom batten

If the wall is plastered, leave the plaster in position if it is sound; use a hammer and cold chisel to chip off slight humps. But if plaster is broken or coming away from the wall, chip it away.

Before you start Check the wall surface to see if it is true and straight. If not, find and mark the part of the wall surface that sticks out furthest so that the timber frame can be made to accommodate it.

Tools *Pencil or chalk; plumb line; steel tape measure; hammer or screwdriver; handsaw; padsaw; drill and twist bits; portable workbench. Possibly also: trimming knife; countersink bit; masonry bit.*

Materials *Sawn timber battens 25 x 50mm – all treated with wood preservative; masonry nails or hammer-in fixings at least 10mm longer than the combined thickness of the batten and plaster (if any); hardboard slivers for packing pieces; plasterboard; plasterboard nails. Possibly also: insulation material and tacks, drawing pins or adhesive.*

1 Lay a framing batten on its side flat against the base of the wall and mark its thickness, with pencil or chalk, along the floor for the whole length of the wall to be lined.

2 Take a batten of the same height as the wall and hold it vertical, flat against one end of the wall to be lined.

3 Using a spirit level or plumb line to keep the batten vertical, move it along the wall and mark any position where its base is outside the line marked on the floor.

On a plastered wall, any obvious plaster humps can be chipped away.

4 At the outermost floor mark, draw a second line along the floor parallel with the first.

5 Using a plumb line and timber batten, mark a line along the ceiling in line with the second floor line.

6 Use masonry nails or countersunk hammer-in fixings at about 500mm intervals to fix a horizontal batten to the base of the wall 25mm above the floor.

7 Align the outer edge of the batten with the second floor line, placing hardboard packing pieces between the batten and the wall where necessary.

MAKING FIXINGS TO DRY-LINED WALLS

Dry-lined walls have a cavity 25–40mm wide between the lining and the solid masonry behind. How you make a fixing depends on the load to be supported. For lightweight items you can use plastic or metal screw-in fixings (below), as for partition walls. Medium-weight items need a cavity anchor, but the cavity depth restricts the types of fixing you can use. Heavyweight items must be supported on fixings made into the masonry using a long screw and wallplug. The best type is a frame plug long enough to pass through wall cladding and cavity, and penetrate masonry by about 40mm.

Making the fixing

Use a twist drill to match the diameter of the frame plug to make a hole in the wall cladding at the fixing location. Then switch to a long masonry drill bit of the same size and wrap tape round it to indicate the total drilling depth (cladding plus cavity plus 40mm). Select hammer action if your drill has it and a slow speed.

1 Insert the masonry drill bit through the hole in the wall cladding and check that it is at right angles to the surface.

2 Drill the hole to the depth indicated by your tape depth stop. Withdraw the drill bit from time to time to clear the hole of debris, which will fall into the cavity.

3 Insert the frame plug and check that its flange fits flush with the surface of the wall cladding. Pass the screw through what you are fixing and drive it into the plug.

8 Fit a horizontal batten to the top of the wall, against the ceiling, in the same way.

9 Use a plumb line to check that the two horizontal battens are in line. Adjust the position of the top batten if necessary.

Fixing the vertical battens

1 Measure and draw lines down the wall where the edges of boards will meet. Vertical battens will be fixed centrally on these lines.

2 Mark the positions of the intermediate vertical battens (which will lie at board centres) midway between the edge battens.

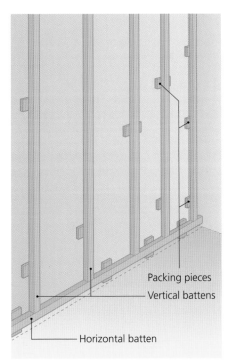

Packing pieces
Vertical battens
Horizontal batten

3 Cut vertical battens to length to fit snugly between the horizontal battens.

4 Fit the vertical battens for the plasterboard edges in the positions marked. Before driving the fixings fully home, use a plumb line to check that each batten is vertical and in line with the horizontal top and bottom battens. Pack behind the batten where necessary (see above).

5 When you are satisfied, drive the fixings fully home.

6 Fit the intermediate vertical battens in the same way as the board-edge battens, using packing wherever necessary.

7 Fix battens all round window and door openings. Make sure they align horizontally and vertically with the other battens.

8 If necessary, put a short length of batten round electrical outlets to support board edges.

9 If there are to be any fixtures such as wall cupboards, fix extra battens at anchor points in the required positions. Mark a horizontal line along the centre of the batten and the adjoining studs as a guide for fixings. Transfer it to the plasterboard when fitting.

10 If insulation materials, such as rigid polystyrene boards or glass-fibre batts, are being fitted, wedge them in place between the battens.

Fixing plasterboard to the frame

1 Cut the plasterboard to leave a gap of 13mm between the base and the floor – the board will hang 13mm below the horizontal batten.

2 Nail the board to the battens with plasterboard nails in the same way as for building a stud partition. Then fill in the joints between boards.

Insulating hot and cold water pipes

Water pipes should be lagged to reduce heat loss and to avoid winter freeze-ups.

Before you start Concentrate first on pipes that run across a loft, above an insulated floor, and those that run along outside walls in unheated rooms. Overflow and vent pipes that are exposed to the cold should also be lagged. Some pipes are boxed in. To lag them, unscrew the box and stuff pieces of glass-fibre insulation all round the pipes. Make sure all pipes are clean and dry before you start.

Lagging pipes with self-adhesive foam wrap

Tools *Scissors.*

Materials *Rolls of self-adhesive foam wrap.*

Self-adhesive foam wrap is useful where there are many bends in the pipes and it would be difficult to use flexible foam tubes.

1 For pipes in the loft, begin work at the cistern. Cut pieces of foam wrap to a workable length with scissors.

2 Wrap foam round the pipe, making generous overlaps of about one-third of the width of the wrap. Take care to cover the pipe well at bends – these are the vulnerable areas most likely to freeze.

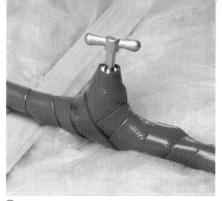

3 Take the wrap around any valves or stoptaps as you meet them, leaving only the handle exposed.

Lagging pipes with flexible foam tube

Tools *Scissors; serrated knife.*

Materials *Foam tube to match pipe size; adhesive tape; plastic clips.*

1 Lag the pipes leading from the cistern first, if you are insulating pipes in the loft. Wrap plastic adhesive tape around the first tube to hold it in place, even if the tube is one of the self-locking types. Push it up tight against the cistern so that the tank connector joint is covered.

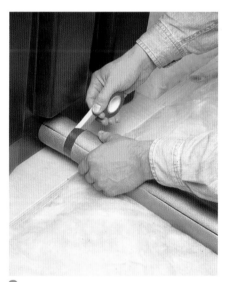

2 Butt-join the tubes where they meet and wrap around the join to hold them tight. Cut the tube at 45° to fit it round elbows and T-fittings, and tape the joints. Alternatively, secure joints with plastic clips.

3 Cut the tube to fit around the body of a gatevalve as closely as possible.

Choosing pipe insulation material

Insulating pipes is critical to prevent them from freezing and bursting in very cold weather, and to minimise heat lost as hot water travels around the system.

Self-adhesive foam wrap Thin foam insulating wrap, 50mm wide, is supplied in rolls usually 5m or 10m long. Some types have a metallic finish.

There is no formula for estimating how much wrap to buy – it depends on the size of the pipes and how large you make the overlaps. Buy and use one or two packs, then work out how much more you will need to complete the job.

Before you fix the lagging, make sure that the pipes are clean and dry. Peel off the backing paper and wind the material round the pipes. Overlap the tape as you wind, especially at bends. This flexible lagging is also useful for insulating awkward fittings, such as stoptaps.

Plastic foam tubes Easy-to-fit plastic foam tubes are split down one side and have to be eased open to fit them round the pipe. They are secured with adhesive tape wrapped round at intervals, or with purpose-made clips. Tubes are available to fit 15mm, 22mm and 28mm pipes. Plastic foam tube is slightly more expensive than self-adhesive foam wrap but is easier to fit.

Foam tubes are available in two wall thicknesses. In most cases the standard grade is sufficient, but if you live in an area that often experiences severe frosts – or if your pipes are particularly exposed – it is worth investing in the thicker material.

Cut neat joints Make 45° cuts in split-sleeve foam tubes with scissors or a sharp bread knife so you can form neat joins at elbows and tees. Use PVC insulating tape to keep the joints tightly closed and avoid a freeze-up.

Glass-fibre blanket Pipes that are boxed in can be insulated by stuffing glass-fibre blanket around the pipes.

COLD-WEATHER CHECKS

• Make sure no tap is left dripping. If that is not possible, put a plug in the bath or basin overnight. Drips cause ice to block waste pipes.

• Never allow cisterns to overfill. Water in overflow pipes can freeze, causing the cistern to overspill.

• In a long cold spell, open the loft hatch occasionally, to let in warmth from the house.

• If you leave the house for short periods, keep the central heating switched on but turned down to the minimum setting.

• If you are away for a long period, drain the plumbing system by closing the main stoptap and opening all the taps. When the water stops running, open the drain valve near the stoptap.

Heating

How central heating works

The efficiency of the central-heating system in your home will be a major factor in your fuel costs as well as overall comfort. The type of system you have may depend on the age of your house. It is important to understand how it works.

A typical pumped system

Most central-heating systems warm the rooms of a house by passing hot water through radiators. There are many ways of heating the water but it is usually through a boiler, which switches on automatically at certain times of day.

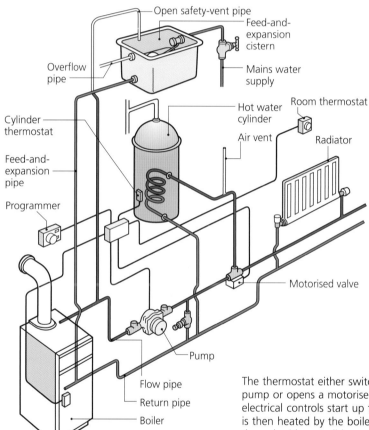

1 A room thermostat turns on the pump (or opens a motorised valve) and the boiler. The pump drives water around the system. The motorised valve opens and closes the circuits to the radiators and hot-water cylinder as required by the thermostats. The water in the central-heating system is separate from that supplied to the hot taps.

2 A programmer switches on the boiler and the pump at pre-set times of the day. A room thermostat controls the room temperature and turns the heating on and off as the air temperature falls and rises.

The thermostat either switches on the pump or opens a motorised valve. The electrical controls start up the boiler. Water is then heated by the boiler and flows through either small bore or microbore pipes to the radiators. When the air temperature reaches the required level, the valve is closed or the pump is switched off.

3 The same water is circulated constantly around the system. In an open system, in case of leakage or evaporation, the water is topped up from a feed-and-expansion cistern. This cistern also takes up the expansion that occurs when the water heats up from cold.

4 An open-ended pipe, called the open safety-vent pipe, provides an escape route for steam and excess pressure if the boiler overheats.

Gravity circulation

In some older central-heating systems and in solid-fuel systems, water is circulated by gravity. When water is heated it expands and hot water weighs less than cold water.

1 Hot water rises up a large pipe from the boiler to the hot-water cylinder. Cooled water descends down the return pipe, pushing the lighter hot water up the flow pipe.

2 A pump, controlled by a programmer and room thermostat, drives water around the radiators. Gravity circulation is reliable as it needs no mechanical assistance, but it requires larger, 28mm pipes. The system is most efficient if the cylinder is directly above the boiler.

MODERN BOILERS

The essential components of a sealed system are now usually housed inside the boiler. As well as saving space because of the lack of a feed-and-expansion cistern, a combination boiler also has the advantage of removing the need for a hot-water cylinder as the boiler heats mains water and delivers hot water directly to the tap.

If you are planning to replace your existing gas or oil central-heating boiler, the National Energy Foundation recommends that you consider a condensing boiler. Although they cost between £100-£300 more to buy and install than a conventional model, this extra cost should be recouped in reduced energy charges in just four years. For more advice on choosing a boiler, see pages 73–74.

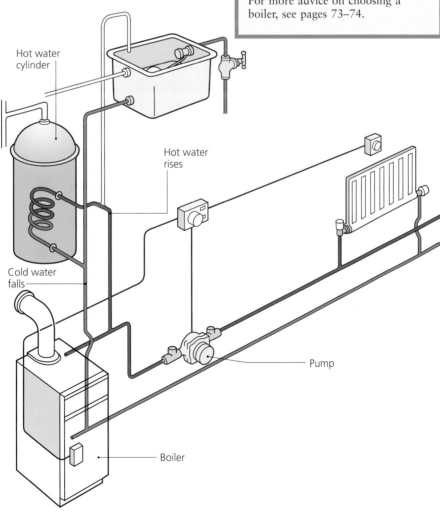

Hot water cylinder

Hot water rises

Cold water falls

Pump

Boiler

A sealed system

A sealed central-heating system has an expansion vessel instead of an expansion cistern, and a pressure relief valve instead of a safety-vent pipe. The valve should be set permanently to 3 bar. Any water lost over time through minor leaks is topped up from the mains supply. Sealed systems are ideal for flats where it is difficult to find space for tanks.

1 A thermostat opens the motorised valve, which controls the circuits to the radiators.

2 The valve turns on the pump to drive water around the system, and starts up the boiler.

3 The boiler has an over-heat cut-out to prevent the system boiling should the standard thermostat fail, and on no account must a boiler without over-heat protection be fitted to a sealed system. It is now more common to use a combination boiler than to build up a sealed system from individual components.

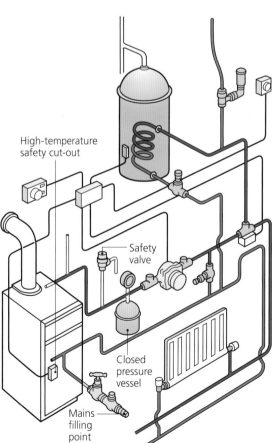

High-temperature safety cut-out

Safety valve

Closed pressure vessel

Mains filling point

Ways of saving heat

Money is wasted if water is heated and then not used. Inefficiencies in the plumbing system, or inefficient use of heaters, can also waste heat.

Keep hot-water pipes short The length of pipe between the hot-water cylinder and a hot tap is known as a dead leg, because hot water left in the pipe after each use of the tap cools and is wasted. The longer the pipe, the more the waste.

Water at 60°C travelling through a 15mm copper pipe loses heat equivalent to more than 1 unit of electricity for roughly each 300mm of run per week – enough to heat about 45 litres of water.

Where a hot-water supply pipe to a basin or shower would involve a dead leg of piping of more than 6m long, it is wiser to use an instantaneous heater instead.

If you have an electric storage heater installed, position it as near as possible to the hot tap most often used – usually the one over the kitchen sink.

Install a shower Use a shower for daily cleansing and keep the bath for relaxed soaking. A bath uses about six times as much water as a shower – although power showers offer a lot less of a saving. If you don't have a shower, you can always buy a special shower attachment – they are not expensive – to fit onto your bath taps.

Avoid secondary hot-water circulation
At one time, if a shower or tap was some distance from the hot-water cylinder, there was a constant circulation of hot water to it by means of a return pipe back to the cylinder. This ensured that there was no delay in the arrival of hot water to the tap. Because of the heat lost, avoid such secondary circulation, particularly with electric heating.

Insulate the hot-water cylinder A 75mm thick lagging jacket on a hot-water cylinder cuts down heat loss by about 70 per cent. A 140 litre cylinder without a jacket, maintained at a temperature of 60°C, loses enough heat every week to heat about 20 baths. Many modern cylinders are foam-lagged by the manufacturer.

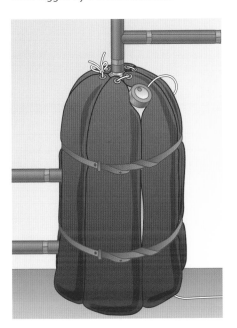

Heat water only as needed Although a thermostat gives economical heating by controlling temperature, even a well-lagged cylinder will lose heat (generally the equivalent of about 6 units of electricity a week). This can add considerably to costs if the heater is left on all the time.

Savings can be made by switching on an immersion heater or boiler only about an hour before hot water is needed, and switching it off when it is not wanted.

KEEPING YOUR COOL

On a hot, muggy evening you may be tempted to switch on one or more electric fans or an air-conditioning unit, if you have one. Instead, turn off as many electrical appliances as you can – such as the television, stereo, DVD player and any lights you can manage safely without. These all generate heat, even in 'stand-by' mode, so will add to your discomfort. And by switching them off you will also lower your electricity consumption.

The most convenient way to do this is to have the heater fitted with a time switch (page 68) that is set to turn it on at times of peak household use. Time switches have a manual override to allow use of the heater at other than the set times.

Take advantage also of cheaper night rates for electricity. Details of off-peak meters and tariffs are available from your electricity supplier.

Prevent scale formation in water pipes and appliances About 65 per cent of British homes – chiefly those in the south-east and Midlands – have hard or moderately hard water. The hardness is caused by a high concentration of dissolved calcium and magnesium salts, and is evident when, for example, soap does not dissolve properly and scale forms inside the kettle and round a tap nozzle.

Hard water drying on any surface leaves a crust of the salts behind and, at high temperatures, the salts solidify into scale. When scale forms inside a domestic boiler or hot-water cylinder it insulates the water from the heat and wastes fuel, and pipes gradually become blocked.

Scale can be prevented or limited by a number of methods:

1 Controlling the hot water temperature – scale starts to form above 60°C.

2 Suspending scale-inhibiting chemicals in crystal form in the cold-water cistern. They need changing every six months.

3 More expensively, by plumbing a water softener into the rising main – beyond the kitchen tap and a branch to an outside tap. This leaves hard water, which most people prefer the taste of, for drinking. Also, it means you are not softening the water for garden use.

4 By plumbing a magnetic water conditioner into the rising main directly above the main stopcock. With this, water passes through a magnetic field so that the structure of the scale-forming salts is altered; they change into fine particles that flush through the pipes instead of clustering together to form scale. The conditioner has a filter that needs cleaning on average twice a year.

Heating water

The average household uses 220–320 litres of hot water a day, so it is worth taking time to find the best – and most efficient – way of heating your supply.

The most common type of water-heating system is a hot-water storage cylinder heated by a boiler (pages 58–59), probably combined with the central-heating system. Various kinds of gas or electric heater can also be used to supplement the system, or installed for use as a complete system in themselves. They may be fed either by a low-pressure supply from the cold-water cistern or by a high-pressure supply direct from the mains.

In flats and other situations where there is no room for a hot-water storage cylinder, a combination gas boiler can provide instantaneous hot water for numerous taps around the house.

Where there is no cold-water storage cistern, un-vented hot-water cylinders are available and store hot water at mains pressure. They are supplied by water heated by a conventional boiler and, because the hot water is delivered at mains pressure, they give good water power to showers without the use of a pump.

Choosing a hot-water cylinder

When choosing a hot-water storage cylinder, make sure that it is an appropriate size for the size of and number of people in your house. Routinely heating more hot water than you can use is the domestic equivalent of overfilling the kettle each time you make a single cup of tea. It is also vital to keep the water hot in the cylinder for as long as possible, as this will minimise your reliance on 'boosts' of top-up heat from less efficient supplementary electric heaters, such as immersion heaters, and will help to cut down the need for a second heating cycle to provide hot water for use during the evening.

Modern hot-water cylinders have built-in insulation, sprayed onto the copper cylinder during manufacture (see page 61), but if you can see the bare metal of your cylinder, buy and fit a lagging jacket as soon as possible.

Immersion heater

An electric element fitted into a standard storage cylinder will heat water fast –

depending on its power rating: 1kW, 2kW or 3kW – on demand, but this heating option is expensive to use unless the storage cylinder is well insulated.

There are three common types of immersion heater: top-entry with one element extending almost to the cylinder bottom; top-entry with two elements – a long one for cheap night electricity and a short one for heating a small amount of water; and side-entry, usually with a pair of elements, one at the bottom to heat the entire cylinder and one at the top, where hot water is drawn off, for heating small amounts. Only water above the level of the element is heated.

All types have thermostats, which are set to the required water temperature. They can be fitted into a copper hot-water cylinder as the sole means of heating or as a supplement to a boiler.

The units can be renewed if the element burns out. Modern cylinders usually have 32mm or 57mm bosses in the dome or low in a side wall (or both) for heater fitting.

Electric storage heater (low-pressure type)

A large-capacity, heavily insulated storage cylinder supplied from the cold-water storage cistern provides hot water that is heated by one or two immersion heaters fitted horizontally.

When two heaters are used, the upper one can be kept on for a permanent hot water supply and the lower one turned on for extra heat when a large volume is needed, such as for a bath. These storage heaters can be installed at any convenient point to supply a number of hot taps, but they must have a vent pipe to the cold-water cistern to prevent them from overflowing as the water heats and expands.

There are compact types of heater for fitting under a sink and larger, floor-standing options, which are well insulated and designed to heat the water with off-peak electricity supplies and keep it hot for use throughout the day.

Electric storage heater (cistern type)

Cistern-type storage heaters usually have a medium or large capacity. They are heavily insulated and supplied from the rising main through a built-in cold-water cistern. The cylinder is heated by one or two immersion heaters, in the same way as a low-pressure type. These storage heaters are useful for supplying a number of hot taps where the water supply is direct from the mains and where a combination boiler (see page 73) is not fitted. The built-in cistern feeds the heater only – no other cold taps.

There are wall-mounted types or floor-standing types. Large, well-insulated storage heaters that are positioned standing on the floor are designed for use with cheaper off-peak electricity supplies.

Instantaneous gas heater

Like a combination boiler, the water is heated by gas as it flows through small-bore copper tubing, but these heaters are for hot water only, and do not supply a central heating system. When a hot tap is turned on, the gas jets are ignited by a pilot light that burns continuously. The jets go out when the tap is turned off.

Large, multipoint heaters can supply all household hot taps; smaller single-point types supply one tap only. The water supply is normally direct from the rising main. The heater can be fed from a cold-water cistern if it is high enough – usually at least 2m above the highest tap – to give enough pressure.

This is a useful option where there is no cold-water storage cistern. Only the water used is heated – there is no slow cooling of unused water. But the delivery rate is slower than from a cylinder, and the flow from one hot tap is interrupted if another is turned on. It is designed to raise water temperature by about 26°C, so in cold weather – when mains water can be near freezing – the heated water is either cool or slow running. In summer it may be too hot. Some have a winter/summer setting to vary the heat.

The heater has a flue and must be fitted against an outside wall for venting.

Instantaneous open-outlet electric heater

A small electric heater, supplied direct from the rising main, heats the water on demand as it passes through. Heaters with a 7kW element are designed for showers; those with a 3kW element for washing hands. Both are designed to be single-point heaters, supplying hot water only where they are fitted, not to a system of taps. The water emerges through a spray nozzle and these heaters are useful for providing a shower where there is no suitable storage cistern supply or for hot water for washing hands in a cloakroom that has no hot-water supply pipes.

As with instantaneous gas heaters, these electric heaters usually raise the water temperature by about 26°C, so the heat varies according to the mains water temperature. Some types have a winter/summer setting to allow for seasonal changes in the starting temperature.

Solar water heating

Generating heat for a hot-water system through solar panels is an efficient option for most homes. The conventional hot-water system is retained as a back-up, but you may be surprised at how little you need to use it.

Solar water heating systems do not directly heat the water you will use, but use the sun's energy to heat liquid in a series of tubes, which then passes through a coil in the hot-water cylinder to heat the water inside. Vacuum-tube or evacuated-tube systems are more efficient than the cheaper flat-plate options and are a better choice for the British climate, as they are unaffected by cold outdoor temperatures and will work even on a cloudy, overcast day. A controller automatically switches on a pump to circulate the heat-transfer fluid in the system whenever the conditions are appropriate, but a second heating coil in the hot-water cylinder is linked to a conventional boiler system for times when solar power cannot meet the demand.

Setting up the system
On average, you will need around one 0.7–1m² panel for each person in the household. Set-up costs are high – up to £6000 for an evacuated tube system – but a solar water heating system used with a gas-powered back-up should pay for itself in energy savings in ten to fifteen years. If the solar system replaces a more expensive-to-run electric water-heating system the payback will be faster.

As with photovoltaic solar panels used for generating electricity (see page 24), solar panels for heating water, or 'collectors', are commonly installed on the roof of the house. Choose a sunny, south-facing spot that receives the maximum amount of sunlight possible throughout the day. Panels are best installed at an angle to catch the sun's rays; angled brackets are available for flat roofs. Remember that solar panels are heavy: take professional advice to be sure that your roof structure is strong enough to bear the additional weight.

Position your hot-water storage tank as close as possible to the solar panels to minimise the potential for heat loss as the heat-transfer liquid travels through pipes between the two.

How much energy can you save?
At a conservative estimate, solar heating can supply 50 per cent of your household's hot water requirements over the course of a year – perhaps as much as 90 per cent in summer – but there are ways to make the most of the free heating to keep your use of the back-up supply to a minimum.

Try to avoid drawing off large quantities of hot water late in the afternoon or evening, as there will be little sunlight to heat the replenished tank of water and you will be more likley to need a boost of heating from your conventional source. Shower or take baths in the morning so that the sun can heat the replacement water throughout the day and the insulated tank will keep it hot until it is needed the following morning.

Don't set your hot-water thermostat too high: 60°C is a comfortable maximum water temperature and one that is easily achieved by your solar system. To make the water hotter than that you are likely to need to use your supplementary heating resource.

Having central heating installed: a checklist

As well as looking at all the central-heating options to see which one suits your household best, ask your heating contractor for information on energy efficiency options and grants available.

Boilers, heat emitters and controls

Read pages 68-74 first, and then gather further information on boilers and heat emitters. You can get additional information from the advisory bodies and trade associations listed here. It is also worth paying a visit to your local plumbers' merchant and picking up brochures on the latest boilers and heat emitters.

Getting quotations

Find three CORGI registered contractors in your area and ask them to quote. Give them all the same outline brief, including where you would like radiators positioned and what temperatures you wish to achieve in the rooms. A living room temperature of 21°C when the temperature outside is –1°C is normal. If you need a margin built in for extra cold weather you should say so. Make a list of any other requirements you feel are important.

1 Be wary of paying a deposit. The first payment should be when materials are delivered. Retain a small amount of the balance (2 per cent) for faults that need fixing after completion.

2 Ask the contractor to give start and completion dates.

3 Before the job starts, decide where pipes are to run and in what order they will be laid so that you can clear the room. If you want pipes to be concealed, state this before the work starts. It will cost more than surface-mounting but is well worth the expense.

4 If several rooms will be affected, ask the contractor to finish in one room before starting in the next one.

5 Your home should be left clean and tidy at the end of each day and should be respected – for example, there should be no loud music or smoking.

6 Work should comply with statutory requirements, such as water supply regulations, the Building Regulations and all relevant codes of practice. Materials must meet the requirements of CEN (European) or British Standards where applicable.

7 'Making good' means filling in holes and replacing panels. Floorboards should be screwed back down to prevent creaking. Damaged boards should be replaced. Normally, however, making good does not include decoration.

8 Establish what other contractors will be required to help to complete the work – electricians, for example.

TRADE ASSOCIATIONS AND INDUSTRY BODIES

Association of Plumbing and Heating Contractors
14 Ensign House, Ensign Business Centre, Westwood Way, Coventry CV4 8JA
tel: 02476 470626
www.aphc.co.uk

CORGI
1 Elmwood, Chineham Park, Crockford Lane, Basingstoke, Hampshire RG24 8WG
tel: 0870 401 2200
www.trustcorgi.com

Heating and Hotwater Industry Council
36 Holly Walk, Leamington Spa, Warwickshire CV32 4LY
tel: 0845 600 2200
www.hhic.co.uk

Heating and Ventilating Contractors' Association
Esca House, 34 Palace Court, London W2 4JG
tel: 020 7313 4900
www.hvca.org.uk

The Institute of Plumbing and Heating Engineering
64 Station Lane, Hornchurch, Essex RM12 6NB
tel: 01708 472791
www.iphe.org.uk

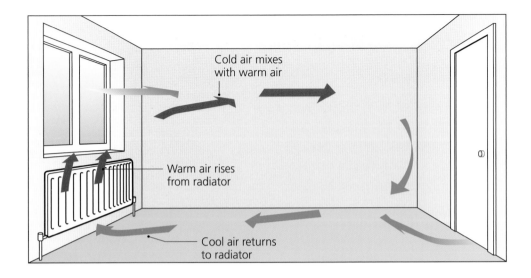

Cold air mixes
with warm air

Warm air rises
from radiator

Cool air returns
to radiator

Where to install radiators

To heat your home as efficiently as possible, it is important to get the maximum heat from the minimum number of radiators. Siting them correctly in each room can go a long way to achieving maximum efficiency. Consider the following points when deciding where to position radiators.

1 Radiators should be fitted in the coldest part of the room, preferably under the windows. The heat rising from the radiator will counteract the cold air falling from the glass. This produces a flow of air across the room.

2 Radiators placed on inside walls opposite a window can accentuate the flow of cold air down a window and can produce a cool draught across the floor.

3 Make sure that there is at least 100mm of space between the bottom of a radiator and the floor to allow a good circulation of air and so that the floor can be cleaned.

4 At least 40mm should be left between the wall – or the skirting board – and the back of the radiator to allow air to circulate.

5 A shelf should not be placed any closer than 50mm to the top of a radiator for the same reason.

6 A radiator installed inside a decorative casing – particularly common in hallways – can lose a quarter or more of its output

unless the casing permits a full flow of air over all of the radiator's surfaces.

7 Do not allow heavy curtains to hang in front of the radiator when they are closed, as they will trap the heat between the curtain and window. Choose curtains that stop just below the window sill; tucking them behind the radiator when you draw them will inhibit the flow of air around and behind it.

When the work is finished

The contractor must flush out the new central-heating system in order to remove debris that could corrode and clog it in the future. He should then run the system to full heat and check that all the radiators heat up.

The contractor must leave you all instructions and technical leaflets, and fill out guarantee cards.

KEEP AWAY FROM THE WALL

Old-fashioned column radiators can be floor mounted, making it easy to allow a good air gap between them and the wall for circulation. They are screwed firmly to the floorboards to prevent movement loosening the plumbing joints, so fitted carpets must be cut neatly around their feet.

Protecting a system against corrosion

The life and efficiency of a central-heating system can be increased by adding a corrosion and scale inhibitor.

Before you start Test the water in the system every year or so for signs of internal corrosion. To do this, drain a sample of the heating system water into a jar and place two bright (not galvanised) wire nails in the jar. Screw the lid on. Wait for a week.

If the nails rust and the water turns a rusty orange (as above), this indicates serious corrosion and you must eliminate the problem as soon as possible. If the water remains fairly clear and the nails do not rust, then no further action is necessary, since the water in the system has lost its free oxygen. A few black deposits are acceptable.

Finding out where air is entering the system

The most common cause of corrosion is air in the system. If the radiators need bleeding more than once or twice a year then too much air is being drawn into the system and this must be eliminated.

The most common areas where air gets into the system are a leaking joint on the suction side of the pump, or through the feed-and-expansion cistern.

Leaks around pumps can be repaired in the same way as other leaking joints. But if air is entering through the feed-and-expansion cistern you will need expert help.

You can find out if the feed-and-expansion cistern is the source of the problem by running the programmer through its functions and checking for any swirling movement of water in the cistern.

To find out whether the vent pipe is sucking in air, submerge the end of the pipe in a cup of water. If the pipe draws up water from the cup, then air is entering the system through the pipe and causing corrosion. You will need to call a central-heating engineer to rectify the problem.

Adding a corrosion inhibitor

Corrosion inhibitors are available in liquid form. In an open-vented system the liquid is added through the feed-and-expansion cistern in the loft.

In a sealed system, you can inject the corrosion inhibitor into a radiator through the air vent (below).

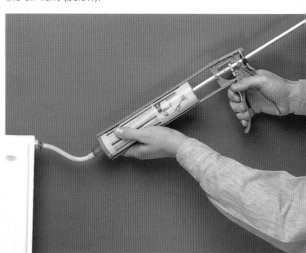

Controlling your central heating

Efficient temperature and time controls can cut heating costs by up to 17 per cent.

Room thermostat This temperature-sensitive switch is set to a pre-selected room temperature. It sends an electrical signal to switch the heating on when the air temperature falls below the pre-set level, and off when it rises above the level.

A room thermostat is best placed in a draught-free spot on an inside wall away from direct sunlight, about 1.5m above floor level and away from any heat sources.

By turning down the room thermostat by just 1°C you can reduce your heating bills by 10 per cent.

Thermostatic radiator valve These valves regulate the flow of water through the radiators to which they are fitted, opening and closing according to the temperature in the room. If the room is cold, a full flow is allowed through to the radiator. Then, as the room warms up the valve closes to reduce the hot water flow through the radiator.

TRVs save money and energy by allowing you to set different temperatures in different rooms. Rooms facing south and rooms with open fires, other heaters or hot appliances, such as an oven, benefit most from TRVs. Most systems are compatible with TRVs. Seek expert advice on which ones to buy.

Programmers Time controls range from simple switches to complex electronic programmers. The most useful can time space heating and domestic hot water separately, so water heating can be turned on and off at the same times of day all year round, while space heating times can vary with the season. Electronic types can give

you three control periods a day and different settings for every day of the week. Some even have a 'holiday' setting.

Combined programmable thermostats give even more energy-efficient heating control. The programmer can be set to maintain different specified room temperatures depending on the time of day. This allows you to raise the temperature in the early morning or at bedtime and drop it to a lower level during the day, when people are dressed and active in the house.

Water heating control An electric thermostat on the outside of the hot-water cylinder will control the water temperature. It operates a motorised valve to restrict the flow of water through the heating coil inside the cylinder. This saves energy because it means that hot water for taps is not heated as high as that for radiators.

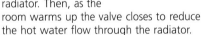

Boiler energy management Sophisticated devices make sure that the boiler works only when needed. A boiler energy manager will reduce wasteful short cycling on a boiler – that is, when 'hot water only' is selected on a conventional central-heating programmer, the boiler will switch on and off continually to keep the water in the boiler at the selected temperature. It will do this even though the hot-water cylinder is already full of hot water. This 'short cycling' can add as much as 30 per cent to fuel bills.

The device will also take account of outside temperatures, and will regulate the central-heating system accordingly. For example, it will override the setting and delay the start time of the central heating on warmer days.

Updating your central heating programmer

An old-style programmer can be replaced quite easily with a more modern, efficient one.

For a modern heating system to run efficiently and provide warmth and comfort at a low cost, you will need a highly efficient boiler and also good controls. While the boiler will ensure that little potential heat is wasted, good controls encourage efficiency as they are designed to ensure that the boiler is working only when it is needed.

Before you start If the old programmer has an industry-standard backplate, the programmer faceplate can be changed without complete rewiring. If the new programmer is incompatible with the old backplate, you will have to do some rewiring. Full instructions will be supplied with the new programmer.

Tools *Electric screwdriver.*

Materials *New programmer. Possibly also pencil; paper; masking tape.*

1 Turn off the power supply to the system's wiring centre and remove the fuse.

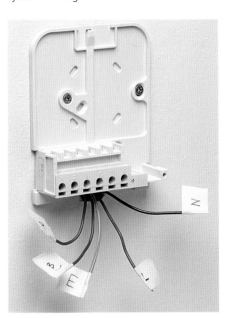

2 Undo the screw securing the faceplate of the programmer. You will usually find it on the underside.

3 Lift the bottom of the faceplate outwards. The programmer will then lift clear of the backplate that is attached to the wall.

4 Set the switch on the back of the new programmer to suit the type of system you have, as described in the instructions.

5 If the new faceplate does not fit the old backplate, study the wiring carefully and label each wire clearly. Sketch the old connections, then disconnect the cable cores from their terminals.

6 Remove the old backplate and attach the new one, using the manufacturer's instructions and your sketch of the old programmer to wire it up.

7 Push the new faceplate into position and restore the power supply to the wiring centre.

IS A BOILER BETTER?

Some people believe that it is cheaper to use an immersion heater to heat water in the summer than your central heating boiler. This is not true if your boiler is efficient, especially when operating at part load. Providing you have a modern, high-efficiency boiler ('D'-rated or better on the SEDBUK scale) linked to a hot-water-tank thermostat, then it will be better to use the boiler to heat water.

Choosing radiators and other heat emitters

Though most people's first choice is a radiator, there are many other heat emitters that can be connected to central-heating pipes. These include fan convectors, trench-duct heaters, skirting heaters and under-floor heaters. When mixing different types of heat emitter on the same system, fit thermostatic valves to each in order to allow full, individual control.

Radiators

Despite the name, only a tiny proportion of heat given off by a radiator is emitted from the front through radiation. If you put your hand just a few inches from the front the heat is negligible. Most of the heat is given out from the top by convection.

To work properly, a radiator must have a good flow of air passing from the bottom on the front and back surfaces (see page 66).

Old style plain panel radiators have now been almost completely superseded by convector radiators, which have metal boxed fins welded to the hidden faces of the panels. They act as chimneys for hot air, nearly doubling the heat output and making it possible to fit smaller radiators.

There are many different styles of tubular radiator available, from modern interpretations of a traditional Victorian style (below left) to quirky, wall-mounted spirals (below right).

Trench-duct heaters

If windows go down to the floor, trench heaters can be installed. A pipe fitted with fins runs along one side of a trench in the floor. A dividing plate along the centre of the trench separates the hot air rising from the pipe from the cooler air returning to be reheated.

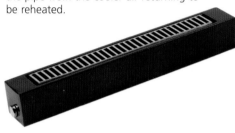

Skirting heaters

Small metal convectors run round the room just above or in place of a skirting board. This system is good for background heating and it gives an even spread of heat, which can help to prevent condensation on walls. However, it is not usually powerful enough to heat a room in very cold weather.

Underfloor heaters Burying pipes under concrete floors has gained in popularity in recent years. Plastic pipe is laid in a continuous loop and carries hot water under the floor. The pipes must be fitted on top of under-floor insulation and are normally covered with a sand-and-cement screed that helps to spread the heat evenly. This is an ideal system for use with a condensing boiler, because it works well at low temperatures. For more information on underfloor heating, see page 72.

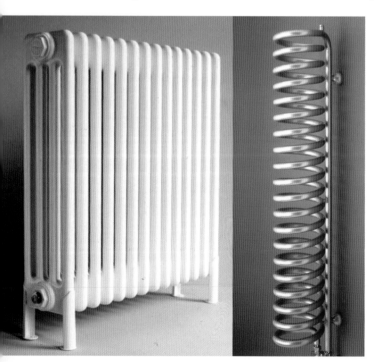

Fan convectors Use a fan convector where there is not enough wall space for a radiator. Special kick-space models are made to fit under kitchen base units (as shown, top right). There are also versions available with low-voltage fans designed for use in bathrooms. Air curtain models can be installed above doors and wall units, and some models sink into the floor.

An electrical fan blows air across copper fins, which are heated by hot water from the central-heating circuit. A filter in the air intake traps dirt. This should be cleaned regularly to maintain maximum performance and to prevent noise.

All-electric kick-space fan heaters are also available to provide heat in a kitchen without linking in to the central heating.

SIZING RADIATORS

To make your central heating system as efficient as possible it is vital to size your radiators correctly, so that you do not fit radiators that are too large for the room and end up heating excessive amounts of water to fill them, then turning them down because the room is too hot. A comfortable temperature varies according to the purpose of the room. The table below lists the average temperatures to aim for in the different rooms of the house.

The size and insulating properties of windows will affect the amount of heat lost from a room and therefore the heat that a radiator will need to generate to compensate, but as a general rule of thumb you can use the following guidelines to calculate the size of radiator you will require.

Estimate the size of the room in cubic feet, multiplying together the length, width and height measured in feet. For a lounge, dining room or bathroom, multiply this figure by 5; for bedrooms multiply by 4 and for other rooms multiply by 3. Add a further 15 per cent for rooms facing north; add 20 per cent if the room has French windows and deduct 10 per cent from the total for double glazing. Your final figure is the required output in BTUs (British Thermal Units) for a radiator to heat the room.

Converting BTUs to Watts

Radiators are sometimes sold with their heat output quoted as Watts, rather than BTUs. To convert your BTU calculation to an equivalent Watt rating, multiply the figure by 0.293.

Ideal room temperatures (°C)

Lounge	21
Dining room	21
Kitchen	16
Bedroom	16
Bathroom	23
Stairs	18

Underfloor heating

Underfloor heating warms the entire surface of the floor. Even in a small room, this is a large radiant surface, which means that the heat provided needs to be only slightly hotter than the room and you will use less energy heating the water to run the system.

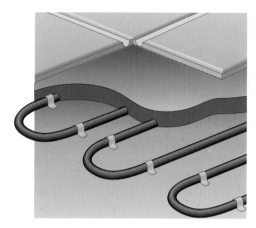

Typically, the temperature of the water in an underfloor heating system pipe is 45–65°C compared to the 80°C surface temperature of a radiator. Most underfloor systems warm the floor to 25–28°C, which is comfortable to walk on. There are two main underfloor heating systems – water and electric. Water systems that are plumbed into your boiler are far more energy-efficient than electric mats.

Underfloor heating: advantages
• Underfloor heating is unobtrusive, freeing up walls which might otherwise have radiators against them. In addition, it is quiet in use. There is even distribution of heat across each room, and individual room temperature control.
• It is safer than other systems of central heating: there is no risk of contact with surfaces that are too hot.
• The electric system is easy to install and requires no special skills.

Underfloor heating: disadvantages
• Heating systems cannot respond rapidly to quick temperature changes, and have longer heat-up and cooling-down periods than other forms of central heating.
• There is greater disruption when installing an underground heating system in an existing building than with other systems.
• The choice of floor finishing requires careful consideration, and changes of floor finish may affect performance.

Water heated systems
Water systems use warm water pumped through small diameter (usually 10mm) plastic pipes which run up and down the sub-floor. The pipes are linked into the building's central heating system. They warm the floor, which in turn warms the room above. Pipes can be installed when the building is constructed or, in some cases, fitted later.

In a new construction (such as a conservatory extension) with a solid ground floor, pipes are laid within the sand-and-cement screed. Insulation beneath the pipework ensures that heat is directed into the room and energy is not wasted in heating the concrete foundations.

On upper floors and suspended wood floors (with joists and floorboards), heating pipes can be laid between the joists. An insulation layer underneath the pipework prevents the ceiling of the room below from getting warm and directs heat to where it is needed: the room above. A water system is best installed by a qualified contractor.

Electric systems
An alternative to a wet system is an electric system. This is easier to fit, and is a more realistic DIY option, but is more expensive to run. An electric mat, similar in appearance to an electric blanket, is laid on the floor, and your chosen floor covering laid on top.

Many companies supply their products to both the trade and DIY consumer, and most have technical departments that supply installation instructions and even check the completed system.

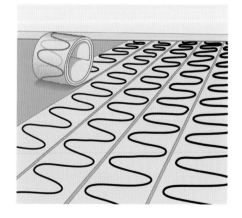

Choosing a boiler

Selecting an appropriate boiler for your household needs will reduce energy wastage and keep fuel costs down. Consider whether it will be supplying heating and hot water, the size of your family and how many bathrooms you need to service.

When choosing a boiler
• Its proposed position affects whether you need a wall-hung or floor-standing model. The boiler's distance from an outside wall or the roof will affect the type of flue you have (see page 74).
• Boilers are available for all types of fuel – oil, gas, LPG (liquefied petroleum gas), solid fuel and even electricity. Gas is the most common, followed by oil and LPG for homes with no gas supply. Oil and gas have similar running costs and are cheaper than LPG. Oil and LPG require storage tanks.
• Consider the space available – not just for the boiler, but also for a hot water cylinder and cold water tanks, and what the demands on the system are likely to be.
• Look for energy rating labels to compare running costs. Remember that some boilers need more maintenance than others.
• All boilers most be serviced regularly and faults dealt with by an expert. A new or replacement boiler must now meet Building Regulation requirements. This demands a minimum efficiency (of 78 per cent for gas boilers, 80 per cent for LPG and 85 per cent for oil) and it should be installed by a CORGI or OFTEC engineer. Programmers and thermostats must be installed, too.

Conventional boiler The gas or oil-burner heats water in a heat exchanger, rather like a gas-ring under an old-fashioned kettle. Traditionally, heat exchangers have been made from cast-iron, but lighter aluminium and stainless steel are more commonly used now. Most modern, conventional boilers are wall-hung with balanced flues, but floor-standing models with conventional flues are still available. Most conventional boilers are designed for used on fully-pumped open-vented systems; a few will work with existing gravity hot-water systems.

Combination boiler Also known as a 'combi' boiler, this is a central-heating boiler and multi-point water heater all in one. Hot water for the radiators is heated in its own circuit (usually sealed) in the normal way, but the boiler also heats cold water from the mains, delivering it on demand to the hot water taps around the house. The main advantages are the savings in space – no hot water cylinder or tanks – a constant supply of hot water and better water-pressure in showers. By altering the cold-water plumbing, there can also be drinking water at all cold taps. The disadvantages are the cost of the boiler and low flow-rates if more than one hot tap is being used. Some combi boilers store a little hot water so that it is immediately ready for use. Most can be used with gas or LPG, though oil-fired options are also available.

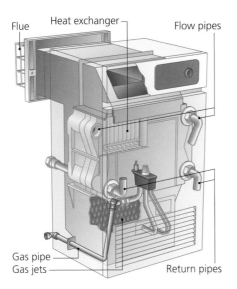

Flue • Heat exchanger • Flow pipes • Gas pipe • Gas jets • Return pipes

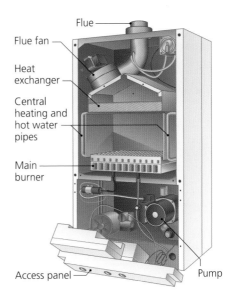

Flue • Flue fan • Heat exchanger • Central heating and hot water pipes • Main burner • Access panel • Pump

Back boiler A back boiler is a heat exchanger located behind a gas fire. Although many still exist in older houses, they are no longer an option for a new fitting for most people.

A back boiler works in much the same way as a conventional boiler, sending hot water to radiators on a central-heating circuit and to a hot-water cylinder, but it needs a conventional open flue, suitably lined for the fuel being used. A back boiler can be used with a fully-pumped system or with gravity hot water circulation. The firefront may be inset into a fireplace or may protrude into the room.

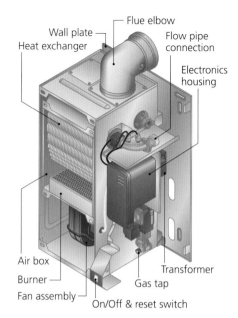

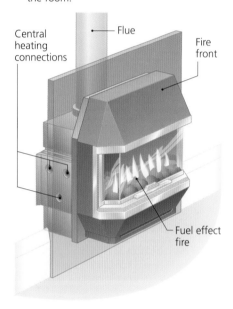

Condensing boiler With a larger heat-exchanger than a conventional boiler, a condensing boiler is designed so that the water returning from the heating system is used to cool the flue gases, extracting extra heat that is normally lost through the flue. Often known as 'high efficiency' boilers, they are meant to be used with a fan-assisted balance flue and in a fully-pumped system. When the flue gases are cooled, water vapour will condense and so a pipe has to be installed to drain this water away.

Condensing boilers work best with lower system water temperatures, but even with normal radiator temperatures, the efficiency will be significantly greater than with a conventional system; this means the extra cost of the boiler is soon recovered in the saving in fuel costs, after which you continue to save money and reduce carbon dioxide emissions. Condensing boilers are available for use with gas, LPG or oil. Combination condensing boilers are available, too.

THE TWO TYPES OF FLUE

Balanced flue
In order to work properly, this two-part duct allows the combustion gases to escape and fresh air to enter. The flue is sealed so that no combustion gases can enter the room where it is installed – it is also known as a 'room-sealed' flue. With a natural-draught balanced flue, the boiler must be installed on an outside wall, so that the flue passes directly through the wall. With a fan-assisted balanced flue, the boiler (which contains an electric fan) can be mounted on any wall, and is conducted by a duct to the flue that can be on an outside wall or can pass through the roof. Fan-assisted balanced flues are more efficient but noisier than natural-draught balanced flues.

Open flue
This can be either an existing chimney that has been lined or a new circular duct installed on an outside wall. The flue will only take the combustion gases, so the fresh air supply for the burner must come from the room. Consequently, special ventilators or grilles will need to be installed on outside walls.

Replacing a hot-water cylinder

Hot-water cylinders are mostly trouble-free but they do sometimes develop leaks or become clogged with limescale in hard water areas, making them inefficient and expensive to run.

Tools *Pipe grips; open-ended spanners; screwdrivers; hose; pipe clips; immersion heater spanner.*

Materials *New pre-lagged copper cylinder; PTFE tape; immersion heater fibre washer.*

Before you start You may have to alter the plumbing if the existing connections do not line up with those on the new cylinder.

1 Turn off the power to the immersion heater, remove the round top cover and disconnect the flex from the terminals.

2 Shut down the boiler and shut off the cold-water feed to the cylinder. This pipe enters the cylinder at the bottom. If there is no gatevalve, tie the ballvalve up in the cold water tank to stop the cylinder from refilling.

3 Open the hot and cold bath taps to drain the supply pipes, but note that this does not drain the water from the cylinder.

4 Attach a length of hose to the drain valve on the bottom of the cylinder (below). Put the other end into a drain, open the small square nut on the drain valve two turns and let the water drain from the cylinder.

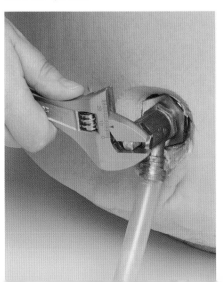

5 Remove the immersion heater from the top of the cylinder by unscrewing it with a special immersion heater spanner then withdrawing it.

6 Disconnect the pipes from the cylinder. Use two spanners: one to hold the securing nut on the cylinder and the other to undo the outer union nut (see below). If you have a Conex style nut use a pipe wrench instead. You will need to disconnect the cold water inlet, the hot water outlet at the top of the cylinder and the connections to and from the heater coil if the water in the cylinder is indirectly heated.

7 Lift out the old cylinder, being careful not to damage the ends of the disconnected pipework.

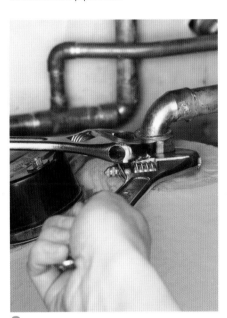

8 Wrap three layers of PTFE tape around the connection spigots on the new cylinder. Lift it back into place and reconnect the pipes, using two spanners to tighten the joint as you did when undoing the old connection.

NEW FOR OLD

Replacing an old cylinder with a new one that incorporates factory-fitted foam insulation will reduce heat loss from the water inside and improve the efficiency of your hot-water system. Choose a new cylinder of an appropriate size for your household.

HOT-WATER CYLINDERS

Connections to the hot-water cylinder

Hot water outlet to hot taps

Immersion heater temperature control

Heat-resistant flex to 20A switch for immersion heater

Immersion heater element

Hot water inlet from boiler

Cold water returning to boiler

Drain valve

Cold water inlet from cistern

9 Refit the immersion heater (pages 77–79). If it was fitted with a fibre washer then replace the washer or wrap PTFE tape around the threads before you refit it. Tighten with the immersion heater spanner but do not over tighten – cylinders are thin and can crease easily.

10 Reconnect the flex to the immersion heater terminals and install the cover (see right).

11 Close the drain valve, then turn on the water supply to the cylinder. Check for leaks as the cylinder fills. If all is well, relight the boiler.

IMMERSION HEATERS

Replacing an immersion heater

An immersion heater element can burn out after long use or if it becomes coated with limescale, which also affects efficiency. Water that takes longer than usual to heat up may indicate scaling. Some immersion heaters are designed to be used in hard water areas.

Before you start Although modern heaters have a thermostat and can be prevented from heating above 60°C – the temperature at which scale starts to form – they may be used as a supplement to a boiler that does not have the same degree of heat control.

To fit a replacement immersion heater to a low-pressure or cistern-type electric storage heater, follow the heater maker's instructions. The heater may be on a plate assembly that can be withdrawn without draining the water chamber.

Tools *Immersion heater spanner – box-type for deep lagging; electrical screwdriver; adjustable spanner; hose clip.*

Materials *Immersion heater; PTFE tape. Possibly also 1.5mm2 three-core heat-resisting flex; penetrating oil.*

1 If the cylinder is heated by a boiler, switch the boiler off. Then switch off the electricity supply at the consumer unit (fuse box).

2 Stop the water supply to the cylinder. Turn off the gatevalve on the supply pipe, if there is one, or drain the cold-water cistern.

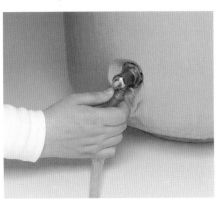

Turn on a hot tap until no more water comes out or attach a hose to the drain valve either on the side of the cylinder or on the cold-water inlet pipe. Run the hose to a drain.

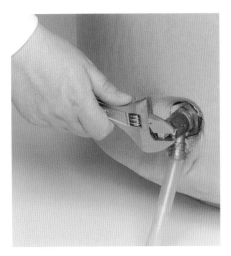

3 Use an adjustable spanner to open the drain valve. If the nut is tight, grip the body of the tap with a second adjustable spanner to prevent it from turning and breaking the seal with the cylinder.

4 Drain water from the cylinder as necessary – about 4.5 litres for a top-entry or high side-entry heater, or the whole cylinder for a low side-entry heater. Close the drain valve.

5 Unscrew and remove the immersion heater cover. Note which of the three conductors is connected to which terminal, then disconnect them using an electrical screwdriver.

HELPFUL TIP

If the heater is difficult to remove, do not force it. Apply penetrating oil round the joint and leave it overnight. Alternatively, warm the joint with a hair dryer, then try loosening it again with the spanner. Do not give one strong pull. Instead, loosen the thread by giving the spanner two or three sharp taps with a hammer in the opening direction (counter-clockwise).

IMMERSION HEATER IN A HOT WATER CYLINDER

The heater may be inserted into the top of the cylinder, and have either one or two elements. Alternatively, there may be one or two separate immersion heaters inserted through the side of the cylinder, one at the top and another at the bottom. The lower one is normally used with off-peak electricity.

6 Use an immersion heater spanner to unscrew the old immersion heater and withdraw it from its boss. A flat spanner is suitable if there is no deep lagging.

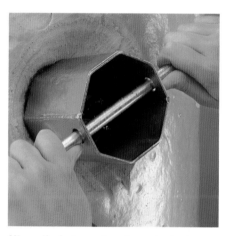

Alternatively For a deep-lagged cylinder, you will need a box-type immersion heater spanner, turned with a tommy bar.

7 If there is no fibre sealing washer supplied with the new heater, bind the thread on the tail of the new immersion heater with PTFE tape.

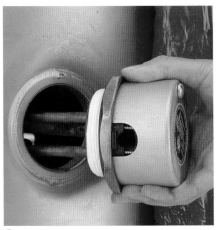

8 Insert the heater into the cylinder boss. In an indirect cylinder, make sure the element does not foul the heat exchanger.

9 Use the immersion heater spanner to screw the heater firmly home.

10 Restore the water supply and check for leaks round the heater boss. If there are any, tighten the heater slightly.

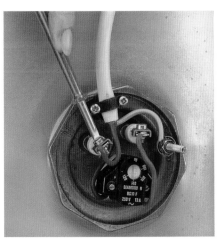

11 Remove the retaining cap of the new heater and reconnect the three electric conductors to their correct terminals. Use new flex if necessary.

12 Set the heater thermostat (see below). Set a single thermostat (or the cheap-rate thermostat on an off-peak system) no higher than 60°C in a hard-water area (to prevent scale forming), or up to 65–70°C in a soft-water area. Where two thermostats are fitted, set the one for day-time operation to 50–55°C.

13 Refit the cap on the immersion heater, then restore the electricity supply at the consumer unit (fuse box).

SETTING THE THERMOSTAT

The temperature control can normally be adjusted with a screwdriver – the settings are marked round the screw. Some two-element heaters have one thermostat, some have two.

Dual (two-element) immersion heaters sometimes have a thermostatic switch unit that can be switched to either 'bath' or 'sink'. Their thermostats cannot normally be adjusted.

IMMERSION HEATERS

Balancing a radiator circuit

If your radiators are not properly balanced, some will get too hot while others remain cool. By balancing them correctly, you can achieve maximum comfort far more efficiently.

Hot water is carried from the boiler to the radiators by a flow pipe, which branches off to supply each radiator. Cool water leaves each radiator at the opposite end and joins a return pipe carrying it back to the boiler. Water flows most readily round the radiators nearest to the pump, so the water flow through the circuit is balanced out by adjusting the lockshield valve on each radiator. The valves are set so as to make it harder for the water to travel through the radiators nearest the boiler.

Tools *Two clip-on radiator thermometers; spanner; small screwdriver.*

Materials *Sticky labels; pencil.*

1 Two or three hours before you intend to start work on the radiators, turn off the central-heating system to allow the water in the radiators to cool down.

2 Open all lockshield valves and handwheel valves fully.

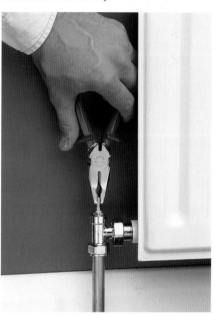

A typical radiator circuit

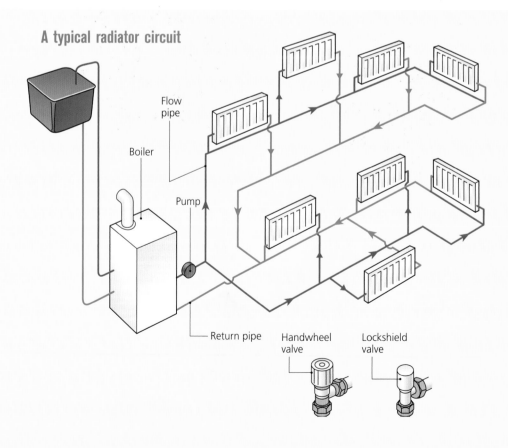

Flow pipe

Boiler

Pump

Return pipe

Handwheel valve

Lockshield valve

3 Turn on the central heating system. Work out the order in which the radiators heat up, and label them accordingly.

4 Clip a radiator thermometer onto the flow pipe bringing water into the first radiator, and one onto the return pipe.

5 Turn down the lockshield valve until it is closed, then open it slightly. Adjust the flow until the temperature of the flow pipe is roughly 11°C higher than that of the return pipe.

6 Repeat for all radiators in the circuit, working in the order as labelled. The lockshield valve on the last radiator will probably need to be fully open.

AN ALTERNATIVE FUEL

Described as the most versatile of fuels for heating, hot water, cooking and many other uses, liquefied petroleum gas (LPG) is perhaps a natural choice where natural gas is unavailable. Delivered in cylinders, there are two types of LPG: butane and propane.

LPG is also used in the automobile industry, and is claimed to be cheaper and cleaner than conventional fuels. In tests, using LPG resulted in 20 per cent less CO_2 emissions than petrol and a 1.8 per cent saving compared with diesel.

Radiator faults

Your heating will not be running efficiently if your radiators are not giving out the maximum amount heat that they are capable of.

Radiator cool at the top

Air is trapped at the top of the radiator. Turn off the central heating. Then use a radiator bleed key to open the air vent at one end of the radiator. Air should start to hiss out. When water appears, close the vent. Hold a rag under the vent to catch the water escaping from it. Turn the heating on again.

If radiators need bleeding more than once a year, air is entering the system and this can cause corrosion. There may be a serious fault that needs expert attention.

Cool at the bottom and hot at the top

Sludge (black iron oxide) produced by internal corrosion can build up at the bottom of a radiator and stop the circulation. Remove the radiator, take it outside and flush it through with a hose. Alternatively, add sludge removal liquid to the feed-and-expansion cistern. Two days later, drain and refill the system (page 85).

Top-floor radiators cold

Cold radiators upstairs only, often indicate that the feed-and-expansion cistern is empty. The ballvalve may be faulty.

Refill the feed-and-expansion cistern so that there is just enough water to float the ball when the water in the system is cold.

Top-floor radiators hot, lower ones cold
This is almost certainly due to pump failure.

Radiators farthest from the boiler are cool
System is not properly balanced (page 80).

Cold radiators throughout
Deposits of sludge caused by corrosion can result in poor water circulation. The system needs to be chemically cleaned out.

Top radiators heat up when hot water only is selected on programmer
Hot water naturally rises above cooler water. On a gravity-driven system, hot water for the hot water cylinder is prevented from creeping into upstairs radiators when the heating is switched off by a mechanical valve, called the gravity-check valve. It is situated on the flow pipe to the upstairs radiators.
    If the gravity-check valve is stuck in the open position, the pipe on either side of the valve will be warm. Call a central heating engineer to replace it.

Leaks in a central-heating system

Never ignore leaks in a central-heating system. Fresh water that is drawn in to replace the lost water contains free oxygen, which can cause radiators and cast-iron boilers to rust. This will cause serious damage to the radiators as well as decreasing their efficiency substantially.

Before you start Internal leak sealants similar to the radiator 'weld' used in cars can be used to seal very minor leaks. Pour the sealant in through the feed-and-expansion tank. Do not use leak sealant in a sealed system.

A leaking pipe joint

Most leaking pipe joints are compression fittings, which can be tightened with a spanner. Tighten the joint slightly, no more than a quarter turn. If this does not stop the leak, do not tighten any further as this will damage the joint.

1 Drain the system to below the level of the leak. Undo the nut on the leaking joint and pull the pipe out slightly.

2 Wrap two or three turns of PTFE tape around the face of the olive where it meets the joint. Tighten the nut.

3 If the leaking joint is soldered, drain the system. Heat the joint with a blowtorch and take it apart, then replace it.

A leaking radiator

A small jet of water from the body of the radiator is called a pinhole leak. It is caused by internal corrosion and can happen within a few weeks of the system being fitted if the debris that collects during installation has not been removed or if air is being drawn in.
    Turn off the valves at each end to relieve the pressure. Then remove the radiator and leave the rest of the system running. Before fitting a new radiator, flush out and clean the system using a non-acidic cleaner.

A leaking radiator vent

If the radiator air vent leaks, drain the system to below the vent. Remove the air-vent fitting using a radiator spanner. Bind the screw joint with PTFE tape, and replace the fitting.

> ### REFLECT THE HEAT
>
> Around 70 per cent of the heat from a radiator is simply heating the wall behind. Energy-efficient radiator panels are available to fit on the wall. These are like tin foil sheets that reflect the heat back into the room.

A leaking radiator valve

If the leak is from the compression joint below the valve, drain down the system to below the joint. Then call a plumber or repair the joint yourself. Use PTFE tape to cure a leak from the union nut connecting the valve to the radiator.

1 Turn off the valves at both ends of the radiator, counting the number of turns on the lockshield valve. Write the number down.

2 Put a towel and a bowl under the valve to catch water, and have a bucket and a second bowl ready.

3 Use an adjustable spanner to turn the union nut counter-clockwise (when looking from the radiator to the valve). Some water may run out.

4 Open the air vent to allow the rest of the water to flow out. Collect it in containers.

5 Wind PTFE tape tightly around the male thread on the valve tail. Start at the end and make a 50 per cent overlap on each turn.

6 Screw the nut back on, and open the valves and air vent. Open the lockshield valve by the number of turns that were necessary to close it. Check for leaks and close the air vent when water flows from it.

> ### WARNING
>
> If there is a thermostatic radiator valve on a radiator, turn it down to zero before disconnecting the tail pieces. Otherwise there is a risk that the valve will open, flooding the room, if the temperature drops.
>
> Alternatively, fit the special screw-down cap, supplied with the valves, in place of the sensor to shut off the valve temporarily.

A leaking valve tail

The leak may be from the valve tail screwed into the radiator. Use a radiator spanner to remove it. Cover the male thread on the valve tail with PTFE tape and replace the tail.

Repacking a radiator gland

If a radiator valve weeps from under the cap, the packing gland is worn. Replace the packing with PTFE tape or thread-sealing fibre, sold by plumbers' merchants. 'Belmont' radiator valves cannot be repacked, but have renewable O-rings.

Tools *Small adjustable spanner; small screwdriver; PTFE tape; silicone grease.*

1 Turn off the valve. If it continues to leak, close the lockshield valve at the other end of the radiator.

2 Remove the cap from the leaking valve and undo the small gland nut. Slide it up out of the way.

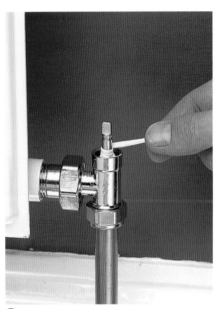

3 Pull a length of PTFE tape into a string and wrap this around the spindle four or five times.

4 Use a small screwdriver to push the tape down into the valve body. Smear on silicone grease and re-tighten the gland nut. Replace the head and turn the valve back on.

Replacing a radiator valve

Although radiator valves normally last for years, you may wish to replace a conventional valve with a thermostatic radiator valve that controls each individual radiator more efficiently.

Before you start Drain the heating system (page 85). As the system drains, open the vents on the upstairs radiators and then those downstairs.

Tools *Two adjustable spanners. Perhaps hexagonal radiator spanner; new adaptor.*

Materials *New radiator valve; wire wool; PTFE tape.*

1 Undo the nut that connects the valve to the radiator by turning it counter-clockwise. To stop the valve rotating, hold the body of the valve upright with a second spanner.

2 Undo the capnut that connects the pipework to the body of the valve, by turning it clockwise (as seen from above). Lift the valve away and let the capnut slip down the pipe.

3 If the new valve is not compatible with the old adaptor, undo it with a hexagonal radiator spanner. Clean the threads inside the end of the radiator with wire wool.

4 Screw the new adaptor into the radiator. It may need a few turns of PTFE tape around the threaded end of the adaptor first to make a watertight seal. Check that the capnut on the pipe can be threaded onto it.

5 Thread the capnut on the adaptor onto the end of the new valve and do it up, finger-tight. Then tighten with a spanner. Brace the valve body with the second spanner as you do this.

6 Slide the capnut up and connect it to the valve.

7 Refill the system and bleed each radiator to get rid of trapped air.

8 Close the radiator vents one by one as the water level rises. Check for leaks and tighten capnuts a little more if necessary.

Draining down the system

Before repairing certain leaks or replacing a radiator valve you will need to drain your system. This is how to drain an open-vented type.

1 Switch off the boiler at the programmer or time switch.

2 Turn off the gas, either at the isolating gas cock near the boiler or by the gas meter. Make sure that the fire in a solid-fuel boiler is out and that the boiler is cold. There is no need to turn off the oil supply in an oil-fired system.

3 Shut off the water supply to the feed-and-expansion cistern. There should be a separate stoptap for this on the branch pipe from the rising main connected to the cistern's ballvalve.

If there is no separate stoptap, or it is jammed and cannot be turned, stop the water flow into the cistern by tying up the ballvalve to a piece of wood laid across the top of the cistern.

4 Locate the drain valve, which may be near the bottom of the boiler. There may be more than one drainage point on the system. Clip a garden hose onto the outlet and run the hose to a drain outside.

5 Locate all the points at which air is vented from the central-heating system. There will be radiator vents, a vent on the primary flow near the hot-water cylinder in fully pumped systems, and manual or automatic vents in the loft if circulating pipes run there. There could be additional vents at other points as well.

6 Open the drain valve with a spanner or pliers, turning counter-clockwise. Water will then start to flow out of the hose at a fairly slow rate.

7 Start opening the venting points at the top of the system. This will greatly speed up the flow from the drain valve. As the water level drops further, open the lower venting points until they are all open.

Refilling the system

1 Close all the drain valves and air vents in the system. Check all work is finished.

2 Turn on the stoptap to the header tank or untie the ballvalve to let water back in.

3 Open one of the lowest air vents until water starts to flow out, then close it. Repeat with the lower air vents until the bottom of the central-heating system is full of water. Repeat with the upper vents, closing them when the system is full.

4 Make sure that the ballvalve to the header tank has closed. The water level in the cistern should be just high enough to float the ball. The rest of the cistern space is to take up the expansion of the water in the system as it heats up.

5 If the water level is too high, close off the mains water supply to the cistern and open the drain valve to let some out. Adjust the arm on the ballvalve so that it closes at the correct water level. Check the cistern's lid and insulating jacket fitted.

6 Switch on the electricity and turn on the gas. Relight the pilot light in a gas boiler. Turn on the system at the programmer or time switch. Turn up the room thermostat.

7 Relight the boiler, following instructions.

8 More venting will be necessary as the system heats up; minor venting will be required for a few days. Check for leaks again after venting the system.

9 Remove the hose from the drain valve, and make sure the valve is watertight. If it is leaking, drain the system again and remove the spindle. The washer is on the end of the spindle. Remove it and replace it with a new one. Use a fibre type in preference to a rubber one because rubber washers tend to bake on and disintegrate.

Removing and replacing a radiator

It may be necessary to remove a radiator in order to flush out sludge that has built up inside, replace it or decorate behind it. This can be done without draining the whole system.

Tools *Polythene sheets; old towels; rags; two bowls; pliers; two large adjustable spanners; absorbent paper; hammer; hexagonal radiator spanner.*

Materials *PTFE tape. For replacement: new radiator the same size as the old one; new radiator air vent; radiator plug.*

1 Lay a polythene sheet and old towels on the floor around the radiator. This could be messy.

2 Shut the control valve by hand. Then remove the cover from the lockshield valve and use pliers or a small spanner to shut it too. Count the number of turns that this takes and write it down.

3 Put a bowl under the control valve and disconnect the union nut. Take care not to distort the pipe. Water will flow out (there may be a lot, so have bowls ready).

4 Open the air vent to increase the flow of water.

5 When it has stopped, undo the union nut on the lockshield valve. Some more water may come out.

6 Block the open ends of the radiator with twists of absorbent paper.

7 Lift the radiator off its brackets and carry it outside. You may need help.

Replacing the radiator

1 If you are replacing a radiator, but keeping the valves, remove the valve tail pieces from the old radiator. Turn the valve tail counter-clockwise (when looking at the end of the radiator).

2 Hold the new radiator in position to check if the wall brackets need repositioning.

3 Wind PTFE tape round the thread of the valve tail pieces. Screw the tail pieces in place.

4 Fit a new air vent at the same end of the radiator as before, using PTFE tape as for the valve tail. Use the radiator spanner to tighten it in. Fit a new plug if there is an open tapping in the other top end.

5 Lift the radiator onto the wall brackets and reconnect the valve union nuts.

6 Open the valves to fill the radiator with water. Let air out through the air vent, and check for leaks. Reset the lockshield valve to its original position.

Relocating a radiator

Correct positioning is essential to maximise the efficiency of your radiators, see page 66 for advice on positioning radiators and follow these steps and those for removing and replacing a radiator (opposite) if you need to move a radiator in any of your rooms.

Tools *Tape measure; pencil; power drill; masonry drill bit; screwdriver; spirit level; hacksaw or pipe cutter; spanners.*

Materials *Radiator; wall mounting brackets; two radiator valves; 50mm No. 12 screws; wall plugs; 15mm copper pipe; compression plumbing fittings; PTFE tape.*

1 Lay the radiator face down and fit the wall brackets into the straps at the back, making sure they are both the same distance from the outer edge of the radiator, and from the base.

2 Measure the height of the brackets, and add 50mm to allow clearance of the skirting board. Measure the distance between them. Then transfer these measurements to the wall.

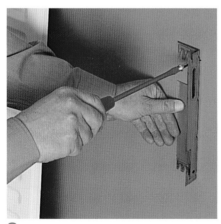

3 Hold the first bracket at the correct height on the wall. Mark the positions of the fixing holes and check that they are vertical. Drill and plug the holes, then screw the bracket to the wall with two 50mm No.12 screws.

WARNING

If there is a thermostatic radiator valve on a radiator, turn it down to zero before disconnecting the tail pieces and removing the radiator. Otherwise there is a risk that the valve will open, flooding the room, if the temperature drops.

Alternatively, fit the special screw-down cap, supplied with the valves, in place of the sensor to shut off the valve while the radiator is out of use.

BOXING IN PIPES

When moving a radiator you will need to run pipework from the old to the new position. If you can lift the floorboards, the pipes can be hidden underneath, running parallel to joists or through holes drilled in them, but if you need to run them above the floor and around the wall you may prefer to hide them.

Make a simple box around the pipes using MDF or hardboard fixed to battens that have been screwed into the wall or floor, or fixed with plastic joint blocks. The box can be painted to match the walls or skirting boards.

4 Position the second bracket at the correct distance from the first and the right height above the skirting board. Fix it with one screw through the long slot, and then check its position with your spirit level before driving in the second screw.

5 Offer up the radiator, slipping the straps on the back over the hooks on the brackets. If the radiator is level, lift it off again and fit the valves. Then replace it and connect it to the re-routed pipework.

Conserving water

Saving water in and around the home

Some simple plumbing adjustments and minor lifestyle changes can make a big difference to the amount of water your household consumes. If you have a water meter you will see savings on your bill, but even if you don't, you will be doing your bit to save the planet.

Recurring summer droughts mean that water shortages are becoming an annual occurrence in many parts of the UK. Hose-pipe bans are the most visible side effect, but pressure on limited clean water supplies can be eased by reducing your usage in the house as well as the garden and by doing what you can to reduce your sewerage output to minimise the volumes of water requiring treatment.

Water-saving WC tips

One third of the average household's water usage goes on flushing the WC. If you have an old WC, fitted before 1993, the biggest thing you can do to cut your water usage is to replace it with a modern slimline model. Old fashioned WCs have 9-litre cisterns, twice the capacity of the average slimline equivalent, and may not have a dual-flush facility. A dual-flush mechanism (below) can be fitted to an existing WC to give the option of choosing a half or full flush by

A WATER-FREE WC

A composting toilet uses no water at all. Instead, the waste drops into a large tank below the floor, which it slowly works its way through. By the time it reaches the bottom of the tank it has degraded into manure that can be used on your garden.

pressing different buttons (below) or holding down or releasing the flush lever as appropriate.

Put a hippo in your tank

Simple water-saving devices – or something as low-tech as a house brick – can be placed in a cistern to reduce its capacity and consequently its water usage. A 'Hippo' will save up to 3 litres per flush in a 9-litre cistern, while an alternate device designed for 7-litre cisterns can reduce the flush by 1 litre each time.

Think before you flush

Consider whether or not you really need to flush each time you use the WC. Fewer flushes can soon add up to considerable savings.

Water-wise washing

Most people know – or think they know – that a shower uses less water than a bath, but in fact, a five-minute power shower can use at least as much water as a soak in the tub, and many people shower under running water for long enough to make the water savings negligible. A five-minute shower with a standard shower uses one third the water of a daily bath, saving 400 litres each week.

Turn off the tap

The best way to minimise your water usage in the shower is to turn off the water while you shampoo your hair or soap your body then turn it back on again to rinse off.

Likewise, always turn off the tap while you brush your teeth and then rinse quickly or with a tumbler of water. Leaving the tap running while you scrub will waste 5 litres of water each minute.

Avoid overfilling

When running a bath, take care not to overfill it – use only enough water to cover your body – and check the temperature of the water as it fills. If you run the bath too hot or too cold, you will need to add more water to cool it down or warm it up before you can get in.

Champagne shower heads

(top right) The latest taps and showerheads incorporate aeration devices, which mix air with the water to reduce the flow without losing pressure – they are sometimes called champagne shower-heads as they put bubbles into the water. Simply switching to one of these showerheads can save up to 50,000 litres of water a year without you even noticing the difference to your daily ablutions.

Choose mixer taps for a lower flow

(bottom right) Fitting mixer taps with a single lever will help to reduce water usage as they mix the hot and cold supplies to achieve the desired temperature, balancing the flow at the same time. Using manual mixers operated from two separate taps is likely to result in a faster flow as you turn up the hot or cold (rather than turning down the opposite) to get the temperature right.

STOP DRIPS

A dripping tap can waste as much as 140 litres of water a week. If the water is dripping from a hot tap, you will also be wasting energy heating water that is dripping straight down the drain. Always fix a leaking tap promptly (see pages 100–105) to minimise the wasted water.

Water-saving tips in the kitchen

Wash vegetables and salad in a bowl rather than under a running tap, if need be just giving them a quick final rinse under a slow-running tap. If you like your drinking water cold, fill a bottle and keep it in the fridge rather than running the tap each time until fresh cold water runs through.

Choose and use domestic appliances wisely

Washing machines use around 14 per cent of the average household's total water consumption and washing dishes accounts for just under 8 per cent. Always wait until your washing machine and dishwasher are full before switching them on: washing two half loads uses more water – and energy – than one full load.

Update machines for savings in water and energy

Consider updating appliances that are starting to get old. A modern washing machine uses only around half the amount of water (and energy) of a machine that is ten years old or more.

When you are buying a new appliance, look for A-rated water-saving models. Many modern machines incorporate 'fuzzy logic' technology, which monitors the size and absorbency of the load and uses only as much water as is necessary. The water that drains after the first rinse is analysed and if it is clear of suds, then the machine will not run an unnecessary second rinse cycle.

Consider the capacity

Don't buy a washing machine or dishwasher that is bigger than you need for your everyday use. It may be tempting to buy a dishwasher big enough to cater for big parties at Christmas and other special occasions, but if there are only two of you in the house for most of the year you will be wasting a lot of water and energy.

Washing machine drum capacities vary and slimline or even worktop dishwashers are available that are big enough for a couple or person living alone. If you are part of a large family, choose the largest you can find – running a high-capacity appliance once will use less energy and water than having to wash two or more separate loads in a smaller machine.

Water-saving in the garden

However parched and yellow a lawn looks during a prolonged period of drought, it will bounce back to lush green health once it rains again after all but the longest and hottest dry spell, so don't be tempted to breach a hosepipe ban in your area and water it.

Even if your region does not impose hosepipe bans, watering the lawn is, in most cases, an unnecessary waste of water. Leave grass a little longer than usual when the weather is hot and dry and this will help it to conserve its own water reserves. Cutting the grass actually causes it to lose moisture and can make it less likely to survive. If you must use a hosepipe, fit a

HOW MUCH WATER DO YOU USE?

Being aware of how much water your individual household appliances use will help you to identify opportunities for making water savings. Do what you can to cut down on unnecessary usage of heavy water users and consider changing your habits to take showers instead of baths, for example. When replacing appliances such as washing machines and dishwashers, look for water-wise models and ones that tailor their use to the needs of each wash. This chart lists the average water usage for the most common appliances and household tasks.

WC
Standard full flush	11 litres
Standard half flush	5.5 litres
Efficient full flush	6 litres
Efficient half flush	3 litres

Shower
Standard shower head	Up to 23 litres / minute
Water-saving shower head	9 litres / minute

Bath
Shallow bath	50 litres
Full bath	150 litres

General use
Washing, brushing teeth etc	18 litres per person / day

Dishwashing
By hand	18 litres
Standard machine	36 litres
Efficient machine	16 litres

Clothes washing
Standard machine	200 litres
Efficient machine	100 litres
Most efficient	50 litres

Outdoors
Garden sprinkler	1000 litres / hour
Washing car with hose	17 litres / minute
Washing car with bucket	30 litres

trigger nozzle so that you can deliver water only where it is needed, rather than spraying wastefully as you move around the garden.

Watering tips

Newly seeded lawns or freshly laid turf must be watered regularly if they are to take root and survive and all new plants must be well watered when they are first planted into the ground or containers. But you do not need to do this from the mains water supply.

Use water butts to collect as much rainwater as you can (see pages 120–22) and use these reserves to water your lawn, beds and containers. Pure rainwater is actually better for your plants than treated tap water and, in hot weather, is usually warmer than that straight from the tap, making it less shocking to the plants.

It is better to soak plants thoroughly but infrequently than water them a little and often. A light sprinkling of water just wets the very top layer of the soil and will encourage plants to grow roots close to the surface, where they are more prone to the effects of evaporation and more at the mercy of the rain. Deep roots can find water far underground even when it has not rained for weeks.

Wait until a plant shows signs of wilting, indicating that its reserves of water are running out, before watering it.

When to plant and water
Make the best use of the water you put on your garden by watering in the cool of the early morning or evening. Watering at the hottest time of day will allow much of the water to evaporate before it sinks in and has a chance to benefit the plants, meaning that you will need to water again sooner than would otherwise be necessary.

If you can, avoid planting new plants in hot weather, when you will need to water them generously for them to settle in. The best times of year for planting new shrubs and trees are spring and autumn, when there is likely to be plenty of rainfall to water them naturally and the temperatures are cooler than the height of summer.

Leave your sprinkler in the shed

A garden sprinkler can use as much water in one hour as a family of four uses in an entire day, so do all you can to avoid using them. Many water companies will insist that you have a meter installed if you intend to use a sprinkler.

Lock in the moisture
Spread a thick layer of mulch around plants in flowerbeds and containers after you have watered them thoroughly. Mulch, whether it is a natural covering of compost, cocoa shells or bark chippings, or a blanket of gravel or other stone, will help to reduce evaporation from the soil, keeping it moist for longer than soil that it left bare.

LOOK OUT FOR LEAKS

A leaking pipe that goes unnoticed can waste many gallons of water. Be alert to signs of leaks in supply pipes into your home. Look out for sudden new boggy patches in a lawn or flowerbed or an unexplained drop in water pressure from taps supplied from the mains.

If you think you may have a leak you can confirm your suspicions with the help of your water meter (see below) or contact your water supply company and ask them to investigate on your behalf. They can run a small camera through the supply pipes to your property to examine the pipes for cracks.

Even if there is no outward sign of a leak, if you have a water meter it is a good idea to check regularly for potential problems. Turn off all the taps and water-using appliances in the house and take a meter reading. Wait for half an hour and then repeat the reading.

If the reading has gone up, then you probably have a leaking pipe. Try to trace and fix the leak or call a plumber or your water supply company for professional help. If the leak is within your boundary, it is your responsibility to fix it, but if the leak is beyond your property the water company should cover the cost of the repair.

Cutting off the water supply

In many homes, only the kitchen tap is fed from the rising main; others are fed from the cold-water cistern. It is important to understand your system so you can carry out repairs.

Taps fed from the cistern

1 To isolate a hot or cold tap supplied from the cistern, turn off the gatevalve on the supply pipe from the cistern. If a service valve (see page 96) is fitted in the pipe to the tap, turn it off with a screwdriver.

2 Turn on the tap until the water has stopped flowing.

Alternatively If there is no gatevalve or service valve on the pipe, you will have to drain the cistern.

Draining the cistern

1 Tie the ballvalve arm to a piece of wood laid across the cistern. This stops the flow from the mains.

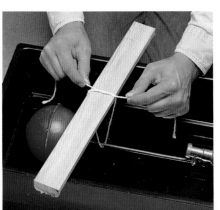

2 Turn on the bathroom cold taps until the water stops flowing, then turn on the hot taps – very little water will flow from them. (You need not turn off the boiler, as the hot water cylinder will not be drained.)

Taps fed from the rising main

Turn off the main indoor stoptap, then turn on the mains-fed tap until the water stops.

Draining the rising main
You may want to drain the rising main to take a branch pipe from it or to repair the main stoptap.

If there is a drain valve above the stoptap, fit a short piece of hose to its outlet and open it with a drain valve key or pliers. Catch the water, usually only a litre or two, in a bucket.

HELPFUL TIP

A stoptap that has been open for a long time may be jammed. To guard against this, close and open the stoptap fully twice a year. After opening it, give the handle a quarter turn towards closure. This prevents jamming without affecting water flow. If a stoptap is difficult to turn, apply a few drops of penetrating oil round the spindle base and leave for ten minutes before turning the handle again. Repeat this process as often as is necessary.

Turning off the outdoor stoptap

You may need to turn off the outdoor stoptap if the indoor one is broken, jammed or has a leak from the spindle. Stoptap keys can be bought from plumbers' merchants, but first check the type needed – the tap may have a crutch handle or a square spindle.

Alternatively If you have no stoptap key, make your own. Take a piece of strong wood about 1m long and in one end cut a V-shaped slot about 25mm wide at the opening and 75mm deep. Securely fix a piece of wood as a cross-bar handle at the other end. Slip the slot over the stoptap handle to turn it. This tool will not turn a stoptap with a square spindle.

1 Locate the stoptap, which will be under a cover, about 100mm across, just inside or just outside the boundary of your property. If you cannot find the outdoor stoptap, call your water supply company.

2 Raise the cover. This may be difficult if it has not been raised for some time.

3 Insert the stoptap key into the guard pipe and engage the stoptap handle at the bottom. Turn it clockwise.

TYPES OF STOPTAP AND ISOLATING VALVE

Stoptap A tap with a valve and washer that is inserted into a mains-pressure supply pipe to control the water flow through it. A stoptap is usually kept turned on, being turned off only when necessary to cut off the supply. It must be fitted the right way round (an arrow mark shows the flow direction). Most stoptaps have a crutch handle.

Drain valve A tap without a handle, opened by turning the spindle with a drain valve key. It is normally kept closed but has a ribbed outlet for attaching a hose when draining is necessary. A drain valve is fitted in those parts of the plumbing system that cannot be drained through household taps – for instance, in the boiler, central-heating system or on the rising main.

Gatevalve An isolating valve with a wheel handle, through which the water flow is controlled by raising or lowering a metal plate (or gate). It can be fitted either way round and is normally used in low-pressure pipes, such as supply pipes from a storage cistern. With the gate open, the flow is completely unrestricted. When it is closed, the seal is not as watertight as a stoptap.

Service valve A small isolating valve operated with a screwdriver. This turns a pierced plug inside the valve to stop or restore the water flow. Normally used in a low-pressure supply pipe to a tap or ballvalve to cut off the water for repairs. A similar valve with a small lever handle and a threaded outlet is used to control the flow to the flexible supply hoses of a washing machine or dishwasher.

Repairing a burst pipe

To prevent water wastage and damage, leaking pipes must be repaired as quickly and efficiently as possible.

As an ice plug forms, it expands and may split the pipe or force open a joint. When the ice melts, the pipe or fitting leaks. Metal pipes are more likely to suffer frost damage than plastic pipes. Copper and stainless steel pipes are less vulnerable than softer lead pipes.

A split copper or plastic pipe can be temporarily repaired with a proprietary burst-pipe repair clamp. In an emergency, a pipe not under mains pressure can be patched with a length of garden hose.

Make a permanent repair as soon as possible. Cut off the water supply (page 96), drain the pipe and replace the damaged length. For a split less than 90mm long in a copper pipe, you can make a permanent repair with a slip coupling.

For lead piping, use a tape-repair kit for a strong repair that will allow you to restore the water supply until a plumber can make a permanent repair (working on lead pipework is best left to a professional).

Using a slip coupling

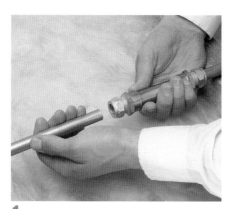

1 Cut out the damaged part and slide the slip end of the coupling (with no pipe stop) onto a pipe end. Then push it onto the other end. If it will not go in, unscrew the backnuts and slide the nuts and olives at each end along the pipe first.

2 Refit the nuts and olives and screw them up hand-tight. Then tighten the nuts for one and a quarter turns with a spanner.

Patching a split branch pipe

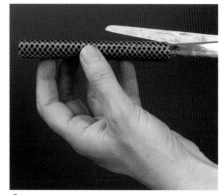

1 Cut a piece of garden hose that is long enough to cover the pipe for at least 50mm beyond the area of damage. Split the hose along its length.

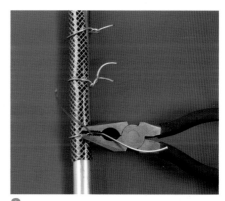

2 Wrap the hose round the pipe to cover the damage and secure it with three loops of strong wire. Twist the loops closed tightly with pliers.

Alternatively Fit an emergency pipe repair clamp and tighten the screws fully with a screwdriver.

How taps work

All taps work in much the same way – a rotating handle opens and closes a valve inside the body of the tap. Traditional taps, such as the rising spindle, use a system of nuts and screws to open the valve, but modern taps use rotating discs instead. A dripping tap left unattended will waste many litres of water. Understanding how your taps work will help you to fix problems promptly and professionally.

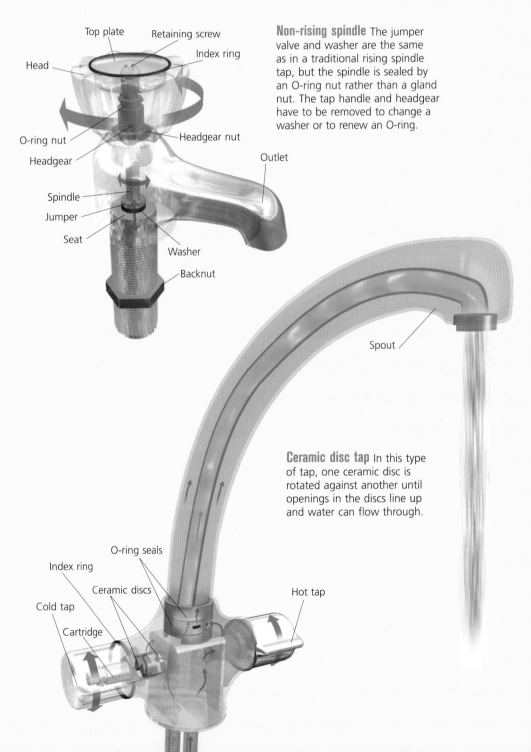

Top plate

Retaining screw

Index ring

Head

O-ring nut

Headgear

Headgear nut

Spindle

Jumper

Seat

Washer

Backnut

Outlet

Non-rising spindle The jumper valve and washer are the same as in a traditional rising spindle tap, but the spindle is sealed by an O-ring nut rather than a gland nut. The tap handle and headgear have to be removed to change a washer or to renew an O-ring.

Spout

Ceramic disc tap In this type of tap, one ceramic disc is rotated against another until openings in the discs line up and water can flow through.

O-ring seals

Index ring

Ceramic discs

Cold tap

Cartridge

Hot tap

Rising spindle The jumper valve is in the shape of a rod and plate, and the washer is attached to the base of the plate. When changing a washer, the handle is lifted off with the headgear. When adjusting the gland nut, the handle has to be removed so that the bell-shaped cover can be pulled off out of the way.

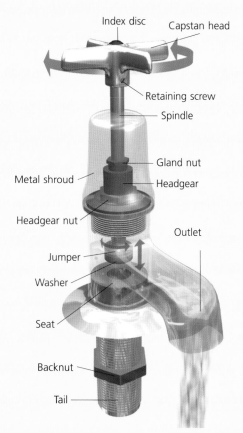

Index disc
Capstan head
Retaining screw
Spindle
Gland nut
Metal shroud
Headgear
Headgear nut
Outlet
Jumper
Washer
Seat
Backnut
Tail

AVOIDING HARD-WATER DAMAGE TO TAPS

If you live in a hard-water area, check your taps for damage once a year. Turn off the mains water supply. One at a time check that the headgear on each tap unscrews easily. Use penetrating oil to release stiff nuts and use a spanner and a wrench wrapped in a cloth to hold the body of the tap as you turn.

If limescale has built up, remove and soak small parts in vinegar or limescale remover. Smear the thread with lubricant before reassembling.

Repairing a dripping tap

A dripping tap usually means that the tap washer needs renewing, but can also be caused by a damaged valve seating. If the drip is from a mixer spout, renew both tap washers.

Tools *One large open-ended spanner, normally 20mm for a 12mm tap or 24mm for a 19mm tap (or use an adjustable spanner); old screwdriver (for prising). Possibly one small spanner (8mm); one or two pipe wrenches; cloth for padding jaws; one 5mm, one 10mm screwdriver.*

Materials *Replacement washer or a washer-and-jumper valve unit; alternatively, a washer-and-seating set; petroleum jelly. Possibly also penetrating oil.*

Removing the headgear

1 Cut off the water supply (page 96). Make sure the tap is turned fully on, and put the plug into the plughole to stop any small parts falling down the waste pipe.

2 Unscrew or lever off the cover of a non-rising spindle tap to expose the retaining screw. Remove the screw and put it in a safe place. Remove the head.

Alternatively With a rising spindle tap, prise off the index disc and remove the retaining screw to release the capstan from the spindle. Use a wrench wrapped in cloth to unscrew the metal shroud and lift it away from the headgear nut.

3 Undo the headgear nut with a spanner. Do not force the nut if it is stiff. Brace the tap body by hand or with a pipe wrench wrapped in a cloth, to prevent the tap from turning and fracturing the pipework attached to it.

4 If the nut is still difficult to turn, apply penetrating oil round the joint, wait about ten minutes to give it time to soak in, then try again. You may have to make several applications.

Fitting the washer

1 Prise off the washer with a screwdriver. If there is a small nut holding it in place, unscrew it with a spanner (normally 8mm). If it is difficult to undo, put penetrating oil around it and try again when it has soaked in. Then prise off the washer.

Alternatively If the nut is impossible to remove, you can replace both the jumper valve and washer in one unit.

2 After fitting a new washer or washer and jumper, grease the threads on the base of the tap before reassembling.

— Washer-and-jumper valve unit

— Plastic seating

— Valve seat

Repairing the valve seating

When renewing a washer, inspect the valve seat inside the tap body. If it is scaled or scored by grit, the seal between washer and seat will not be effective even with a new washer.

The simplest repair is with a washer-and-seating set. This has a plastic seat to fit into the valve seat, and a washer-and-jumper valve unit to fit into the headgear.

When the tap is turned off, the plastic seating is forced firmly into place. It may take a few days for the new seating to give a completely watertight fit.

An alternative repair is to buy or hire a tap reseating tool and grind the seat smooth yourself.

Tap conversion kits

You may be able to get tap conversion kits to change the style of taps and replace worn or broken mechanisms. Newer heads can be changed back to Victorian brass heads, or a tap with a crutch or capstan handle can be given a newer look. The spout and body of the tap remain in place.

Some kits have bushes to fit different tap sizes. The kits are available from most DIY stores and fitting instructions are included.

Cleaning or replacing ceramic discs

Ceramic disc taps operate on a different principle from conventional taps with washers and spindles.

Positioned in the body of a ceramic disc tap is a cartridge containing a pair of ceramic discs, each with two holes in it. One disc is fixed in position; the other rotates when the handle is turned. As the movable disc rotates, the holes in it line up with the holes in the fixed one and water flows through them. When the tap is turned off the movable disc rotates so that the holes no longer align.

Dealing with a dripping tap

If a scratched ceramic disc is causing the leak, the entire cartridge must be replaced: left-handed for a hot tap or right-handed for a cold tap. Remove the old cartridge and take it with you when buying a replacement to make sure it is the correct size and 'hand'. Ceramic taps can also drip at the base of the cartridge if the seal has perished. Replace it if necessary.

Checking discs in a ceramic disc mixer tap

1 Turn off the water supply. Pull off the tap handles (it may be necessary to unscrew a small retaining screw on each) and use a spanner to unscrew the headgear section.

2 Remove the ceramic cartridges carefully, keeping hot and cold separate. Check both cartridges for dirt and wear and tear.

3 If the cartridges are worn, replace with identical parts for the tap unit. Make sure the hot and cold cartridges are fitted into the correct taps.

4 If the cartridges are dirty, clean them with a damp cloth. Replace the rubber seal if it is worn. Replace the cartridge in the tap unit, fitting the hot and cold cartridges into the appropriate taps.

RELEASING THE SPINDLE

A non-rising spindle tap may have a circlip keeping the spindle in place. When you have removed the headgear, lever out the circlip so that you can gain access to the worn O-rings.

Curing a leak from a spindle or spout

Leakage from the body of the tap – round the spindle, the base of a swivel spout or the diverter knob on a shower mixer tap – may indicate a faulty gland or O-ring seal.

Possible causes This sort of leak is most likely to occur on a kitchen cold tap with a bell-shaped cover and visible spindle. Soapy water from wet hands may have run down the spindle and washed the grease out of the gland that makes a watertight joint round the spindle. If the tap is used with a garden hose, back pressure from the hose connection will also weaken the gland.

On a modern tap, especially one with a shrouded head, there is an O-ring seal instead of a gland. An O-ring seal may occasionally become worn.

Tools *Small spanner (normally 12mm) or adjustable spanner. Possibly also one 5mm and one 10mm screwdriver; penknife or screwdriver for prising; two small wooden blocks about 10mm deep (such as spring clothes pegs).*

Materials *Packing materials (gland-packing string or PTFE tape). Possibly also silicone grease; O-rings (and possibly washers) of the correct size – take the old ones with you when buying, or give the make of tap.*

Adjusting the gland

There is no need to cut off the water supply to the tap.

1 With the tap turned off, undo the small screw that secures the capstan handle and put it in a safe place (it is very easily lost), then remove the handle. If there is no screw, the handle should pull off.

2 Remove the bell-shaped cover to reveal the gland nut – the highest nut on the spindle. Tighten the nut about half a turn with a spanner.

3 Turn the tap on by temporarily slipping the handle back on, then check whether there is still a leak from the spindle. If not, turn the gland nut another quarter turn and reassemble the tap. Do not overtighten or the tap will be hard to turn off.

4 If there is still a leak, give another half turn and check again.

5 If the gland continues leaking after you have adjusted it as far as possible, repack the gland.

Replacing the packing

1 With the tap turned off and the handle and cover removed, use a spanner to remove the gland nut and lift it out.

2 Pick out the old packing with a small screwdriver. Replace it with packing string from a plumbers' merchant or with PTFE tape pulled into a thin string. Pack it in with a screwdriver, then replace the gland nut and reassemble the tap.

REPACKING A STOPTAP WITH FIBRE STRING

The gland on a capstan-handle stoptap is the type most likely to need repacking. Use fibre string (from a plumbers' merchant) or PTFE tape.

1 Turn off the stoptap. Undo the gland nut, slide it up the spindle and remove it.

2 Rake out the gland packing with a penknife or similar tool.

3 To repack the gland with fibre string, steep a length in petroleum jelly and wind and stuff it into the gland with a screwdriver blade. Wind and push the string in until it is caulked down hard, then reassemble the tap.

Renewing the O-ring on a shrouded-head tap

1 Cut off the water supply to the tap (page 96) and remove the tap handle and headgear in the same way as for renewing a washer.

2 Hold the headgear between your fingers and turn the spindle clockwise to unscrew and remove the washer unit.

3 Prise out the O-ring at the top of the washer unit with a screwdriver or penknife.

4 Smear the new O-ring with silicone grease, fit it in position, and reassemble the tap.

Renewing O-rings on a kitchen mixer tap

1 With both taps turned off, remove any retaining screw found behind the spout. If there is no screw, turn the spout to line up with the tap body and pull upwards sharply.

2 Note the position of the O-rings (probably two) and remove them.

3 Coat new O-rings of the correct size with silicone grease and fit them in position.

4 Smear the inside of the spout end with petroleum jelly, then refit it to the tap body

Replacing shower-diverter O-rings

Diverters vary in design but most have a sprung rod and plate attached to the diverter knob. When the knob is lifted, the plate opens the shower outlet and seals the tap outlet for as long as the shower is on.

1 With the bath taps turned off, lift the shower-diverter knob and undo the headgear nut with a spanner (probably 12mm size or use an adjustable spanner).

2 Lift out the diverter body and note the position of the washers and O-rings.

3 Remove the knob from the diverter body by turning it counter-clockwise. You may need to grip it with a wrench.

4 Withdraw the rod and plate from the diverter body and remove the small O-ring at the top of the rod.

5 Grease a new O-ring of the correct size with silicone grease and fit it in place.

6 Replace all other rubber washers and O-rings on the base of the rod and plate. Old ones may have to be prised out.

Replacing a WC

Modern WCs with close-coupled cisterns are quite straightforward to install and are much more efficient users of water than their predecessors. First you need to remove the old pan.

Before you start An old WC with a down-pointing outlet cemented to a floor-exit soil pipe is difficult to remove; Newer types are far easier to take out. Start by uncoupling and removing the cistern.

Tools *Adjustable spanner; screwdriver; spirit level. Power drill with wood and masonry bits; safety goggles; club hammer; cold chisel; rags; old chisel; thin pencil; trimming knife; junior hacksaw.*

Materials *Close-coupled WC suite; suitable pan joint (see right); silicone grease. Wall plugs and screws; push-fit tap joint; packing, such as wood slivers or silicone sealant (to level the pan); perhaps nylon pan fixings; toilet seat.*

Removing a pan with a horizontal outlet

1 Turn off the water supply and protect floor with a thick layer of old dustsheets or newspaper. Have an empty bucket to hand.

2 Disconnect the flush pipe by peeling back the cone connector. Alternatively, chip away a rag-and-putty joint with an old chisel. Protect your eyes.

3 Undo any screws used to secure the pan to the floor.

4 Pull the pan towards you slowly, moving it from side to side, to free it from the soil-pipe inlet. It should come away easily. Tip any residual water into the bucket. If it does not come away easily, break the pan outlet in the same way as for a down-pointing outlet (right).

5 If the outlet joint was cemented with putty or mastic filler, clean it off the metal soil pipe inlet using an old chisel. Tape a carrier bag over the exposed soil pipe to keep out the worst of the drain odour.

Removing a pan with a down-pointing outlet

1 Disconnect the flush pipe in the same way as for a horizontal-outlet pan, then undo the floor screws, or break cement with a hammer and cold chisel.

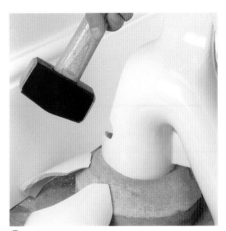

2 To free the pan outlet, put on safety goggles and use a club hammer to break the outlet pipe just above its joint with the drain socket in the floor. Then pull the pan forward, away from the jagged remains protruding from the soil pipe socket.

3 Stuff rags into the socket to stop debris falling in and to contain the smell from the soil pipe. Chip away the rest of the pan outlet with a hammer and cold chisel. If you work with the chisel blade pointing inwards, and break the china right down to the socket at one point, the rest of the china should come out easily.

4 Taking care not to break the collar, chip away any mortar from round the collar of the socket with a hammer and cold chisel.

5 Clear away any mortar left where the pan was cemented to the floor, leaving a flat base for the new WC pan.

Putting together a close-coupled WC

1 Assemble the flush mechanism following the manufacturer's instructions. Be sure to include any required rubber sealing rings.

2 Fit the flush mechanism into the cistern, and insert the cold-water inlet valve assembly. Make sure that its rubber washer is securely in place inside the cistern; then fix in place using the supplied nut. Tighten by hand, then give an extra half turn using an adjustable spanner; do not overtighten.

3 Insert the long fixing bolts through the holes in the bottom of the cistern. Thread bolts through the fat rubber washers and large metal washers supplied.

4 Fit the large rubber gasket (sometimes known as a doughnut) into the flush entrance of the pan or onto the base of the cistern – according to WC manufacturer's instructions.

5 Lift the cistern onto the pan. The connecting bolts will fit through the holes at the back of the pan and the flush mechanism fits through the rubber gasket into the flush entrance of the pan.

6 Thread washers onto the connecting bolts beneath the back of the pan followed by the wing nuts. Hand tighten but do not overtighten, or you risk cracking the china.

7 Carefully move the whole assembly into position.

TYPES OF WC PAN JOINTS

Plastic push-fit joints are now universally used and come in a variety of shapes to allow connection of virtually any pan to any soil pipe. Most joints are either straight or 90° (for horizontal or vertical soil pipes), but offset joints, extension joints and even fully flexible joints are also available.

Angled push-fit pan joint A 90° joint for converting a horizontal (P-trap) pan outlet to a down-pointing (S-trap) outlet for a floor-exit pipe. It can also be used to link a horizontal outlet to a wall-exit pipe situated at right angles to the pan.

Rubber cone joint For linking the flush pipe from the WC cistern to the flush horn of the pan.

Straight push-fit pan joint For a straight link between the pan outlet and the inlet branch to the soil pipe. The cupped end fits over the pan outlet, and the narrow (spigot) end inside the soil-pipe inlet. Different diameters and lengths are made. Before buying, check the outside diameter of the pan outlet, the inside diameter of the soil-pipe inlet, and the distance to be bridged. Joints have watertight seals at each end. Offset types can be used where the alignment is not exact.

Flush pipe Angled plastic pipe linking a separate cistern to the WC pan. Pipes for high-level suites are normally 32mm in diameter, and pipes for low-level suites have 38mm diameters.

Installing a close-coupled WC

1 Choose the right type of adapter to match the existing soil pipe. You will need a straight connector if the pipe passes through the wall immediately behind the pan, and a right-angled one otherwise.

2 You can fix the pan into position with screws – fitted with special inserts to protect the china – or with nylon pan fixings. With the pan in position, draw a line round its base and mark the positions of the fixing holes with a thin pencil, pen or bradawl. If the cistern has fixing holes at the back, mark these positions on the wall, too. Then move the assembly aside.

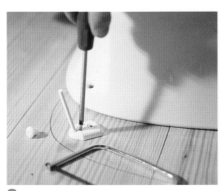

3 Drill and fix the pan fixings so that the plastic thread lines up with the marks on the floor; or drill screw holes into the floor. On a concrete or quarry tiled floor, use a masonry bit and insert wall plugs for the screws. Drill and plug holes in the wall for the cistern.

4 Remove plastic bags or rags from the soil pipe inlet and fit the appropriate flexible connector.

5 Carefully lift the assembly into position using the marked outline to guide you. Position it so that you can slide the pan outlet into the flexible connector. Apply a little silicone grease to help ease it in. If you have used nylon pan fixings, the threads will now protrude through the holes in the base of the pan. Fix the cistern to the wall.

6 Trim the threads to length and screw on the plastic nuts to hold the pan firmly in position. Or push protective plastic inserts through the base of the pan and fix it to the floor with screws. In either case, do not tighten fully, yet.

7 Using a spirit level placed across the top of the pan, check that it is level from side to side and from front to back. Correct the level by loosening the plastic nuts or screws and packing under the pedestal with slivers of wood, or use a bead of silicone sealant. Then screw it down firmly.

8 Connect the cold water supply to the cistern using a plastic push-fit tap joint. These incorporate rubber O-rings for sealing and are simply pushed into place. They can be used to join copper and plastic pipes. Seat mechanisms vary – follow the instructions supplied with your new seat.

Repairing a faulty WC cistern

An overflowing or continuously flushing WC is often caused by a faulty ballvalve, which governs the water level in the cistern.

Checking the water level

1 Remove the cistern lid (it may lift off or be held by one or more screws). When the cistern is full, the water level should be about 25mm below the overflow outlet. Or there may be a water level marked on the inside wall of the cistern.

2 If the level is low, repair or adjust the ballvalve (opposite). If the level is too high and the cistern is overflowing or in danger of doing so, flush it, then repair or adjust the ballvalve.

If the level is correct, the problem is probably with the flap valve and you will need to renew it.

FLUSHING PROBLEMS

The most common problems with WCs are that the WC will not flush, that water runs continuously into the pan or that water runs continuously into the cistern and out through the overflow pipe. Most of these problems are easily fixed.

WC will not flush Check that the flushing lever is still attached to the internal workings of the cistern. Reattach the link or improvise a replacement from a length of thick wire. If the link is still in place, the flap valve may need replacing – this is often the cause if you need to operate the lever several times before the WC will flush.

Continuous flushing When water keeps running into the pan, the siphon may have split or the sealing washer at the base of the siphon may have perished. Both can be replaced. Alternatively, the cistern may be filling too fast, so that the siphoning action of the flush mechanism cannot be interrupted. Fit a restrictor in the float valve to reduce the water flow.

Overflowing cistern Continuous filling may be caused by a faulty float valve or a badly adjusted float arm. Try adjusting the float arm before you replace the valve.

Adjusting the cistern water level

The normal level of a full cistern is about 25mm below the overflow outlet. The level can be raised by raising the float, or lowered by lowering the float.

Understanding ballvalves and water-inlet valve options

If a ballvalve does not close fully, the water level in the cistern becomes too high and causes a constant flow from the overflow pipe. The water inlet of a Portsmouth valve is opened and closed by a washered piston that moves horizontally. The piston is slotted onto the float arm and secured with a split pin. Some types have a screw-on cap at the end of the piston. A detachable inlet nozzle can be changed to suit the water pressure.

The water inlet of a diaphragm-type valve is closed by a large rubber or synthetic diaphragm pushed against it by a plunger attached to the float arm.

Some WCs are fitted with servo-diaphragm valves (also called diaphragm/equilibrium or Torbeck valves). These plastic valves have a small float and short float arm. Behind a diaphragm covering the inlet is a water (or servo) chamber fed via a metering pin. Equal water pressure on each side of the diaphragm keeps it closed. When the float arm drops it opens a pilot hole in the back of the chamber, covered by a sealing washer. This reduces pressure in the servo chamber, and the diaphragm opens the inlet. The outlet is overhead and via a collapsible plastic tube. Failure of any of the parts can cause flushing problems or overflows, but the valve can be fitted with a filter, which collects grit that might otherwise obstruct the metering pin and pilot hole. Flow restrictors in the inlet pipe adapt it for high or low pressures, helping to prevent problems of overfilling and continuous flushing.

Adjusting a ballvalve

Before you start If the cistern overflows, the water level is too high because the float either needs adjusting or is leaking and failing to rise to close the valve (or the valve itself may be faulty).

Tools Possibly small spanner; vice.

On a Portsmouth-pattern valve with a ball float, unscrew and remove the float from the arm. To lower the level, hold the arm firmly in both hands and bend it slightly downwards. Then refit the float. If the arm is too stiff to bend in position, remove it from the cistern and grip it in a vice.

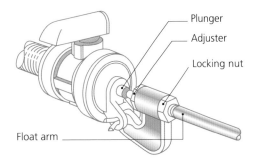

Plunger
Adjuster
Locking nut
Float arm

On a diaphragm valve with an adjuster at the top of the float arm, adjust the level by loosening the locking nut and screwing the adjuster forward, nearer to the plunger.

Alternatively Use an adjuster nut or clip near the float to move the float farther away from the valve along a horizontal arm, or to a lower position if it is linked to the arm by a vertical rod.

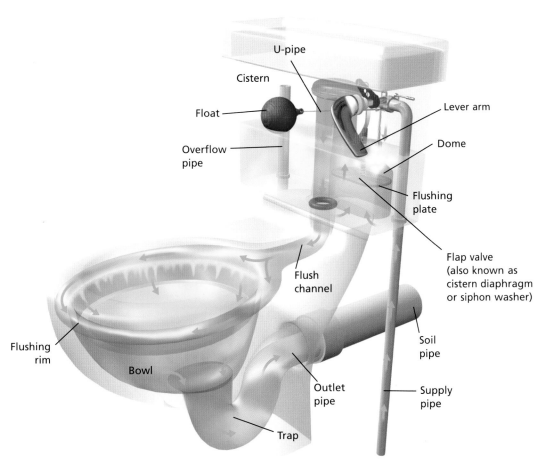

U-pipe
Cistern
Float
Overflow pipe
Lever arm
Dome
Flushing plate
Flap valve (also known as cistern diaphragm or siphon washer)
Flush channel
Flushing rim
Bowl
Soil pipe
Outlet pipe
Supply pipe
Trap

Adding guttering to collect water

Collecting rainwater is one of the simplest ways you can save water, money, energy – and the environment. And it is better for your garden than treated drinking water. From an old dustbin to a water butt or 5,000 gallon tank under your home, it is easy to beat the summer hosepipe ban.

Rainwater falls free of contaminants, so as long as the roof of the building – shed, greenhouse, garaging – you plan to put guttering on is fairly clean and clear of debris, the water can be used untreated in your garden. Installing a 'first flush' device will filter out leaves, dirt and bird droppings that would otherwise fester in the water.

Planning a plastic gutter system

Several similar systems of black, white, brown or grey plastic guttering are available. They differ mainly in the way the lengths of gutter are joined.

Before you start Decide what system you want. In some systems, lengths of gutter overlap and clip into support brackets; with others, a union piece collects lengths of gutter and may or may not have a bracket.

Gutters are rounded or square in cross-section. Most types are clipped onto brackets that support them from below, but some square styles have brackets fixed above them. Five widths of gutter are made to give different carrying capacities to suit the area of roof draining into it. An undersized gutter will not cope with heavy rain. If you are replacing an old gutter system, use the same size as before or a size that is slightly larger.

Measure the total length round the fascia to estimate how much guttering to buy. Measure the height from the gutter down to the gully to estimate how much pipe to buy for each downpipe.

You will need a variety of fittings to connect the parts and hold them in place – for example, union pieces, angled pieces for corners, support brackets, downpipe brackets and downpipe shoes.

Deep gutter Guttering with a deep curve serves large roofs better than the standard half-round type.

Adaptors These will link plastic guttering to cast-iron, larger plastic guttering to smaller sizes, and rounded to square-section guttering. It is not always possible to link one manufacturer's guttering to another's.

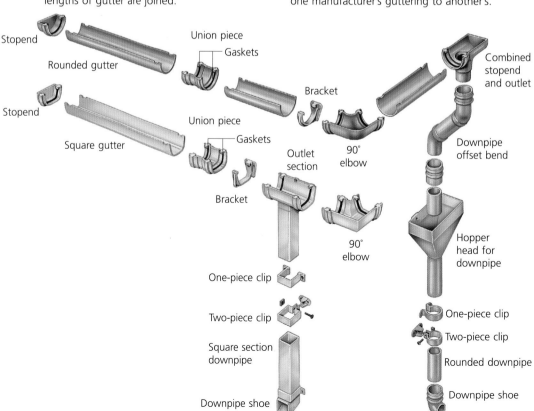

Stopend
Rounded gutter
Union piece
Gaskets
Bracket
Combined stopend and outlet

Stopend
Square gutter
Union piece
Gaskets
Outlet section
90° elbow
Downpipe offset bend

Bracket
90° elbow
Hopper head for downpipe

One-piece clip
Two-piece clip
Square section downpipe
Downpipe shoe

One-piece clip
Two-piece clip
Rounded downpipe
Downpipe shoe

Replacing old guttering with plastic

If your cast-iron guttering is too rusty to repair, lightweight plastic might be the solution for collecting rainwater.

Before you start Plastic guttering is easy and cheap to fit, and requires no painting. Wear strong work gloves as rusty edges can cause nasty cuts.

Tools *Ladder with stand-off bracket; gloves; spanner, hacksaw; nail punch; claw hammer; rope; large screwdriver; small blowtorch; slim masonry chisel; string line and nails; plumb line; steel measuring tape; file drill with masonry bit; pointing trowel; filling knife; paintbrush; chalk. Perhaps a gutter notching tool and a wrecking bar.*

Materials *Plastic gutter; union pieces; brackets with 25mm No. 8 galvanised screws; stopends; gutter outlet section; downpipe; offset bends; solvent cement; pipe clips with 38mm No. 10 galvanised screws; wall plugs; mortar for pointing; filler and paint for fascia board. Perhaps gutter angle; downpipe shoe.*

Removing old pipes and gutters

1 Use a spanner to undo the bolts holding the gutter sections together. If you cannot, then cut through each bolt with the hacksaw, then tap its shank upwards with a nail punch and hammer to free it

2 Give sharp hammer taps at the joints where the sections meet. They will be sealed together with old putty or mastic.

3 Tie a rope round the middle of each gutter section as you free it. Lift it off the brackets and lower it to a helper who can steer it clear of windows and walls below.

4 Try to undo the screws holding the brackets to the fascia board with a screwdriver. If they are rusted in, heat the heads with a narrow blowtorch flame to expand the metal and break the grip of the rust. It the screws still will not turn, prise the brackets away from the board and pull the screws out with them. Use a slim masonry chisel and claw hammer to prise them off.

5 Take out the pipe nails holding the downpipe lugs to the wall. Use pliers or, if the nails are rusted, a wrecking bar to prise the lugs away from the wall. Work down the wall and, as you free each pair of lugs, lift out the section of downpipe from the section below. Use the masonry chisel and hammer to take out the wooden blocks from the wall.

6 If the downpipe goes straight into the ground to connect with a gully, break up the mortar or other surround to free it.

Repairs and preparations

1 Repair the fascia board with exterior filler if necessary, before repainting it. Repair damaged pointing where necessary.

2 Nail a plumb line to drop from the fascia to the gully where the downpipe will discharge. Mark its position with chalk on the fascia and wall, then remove it.

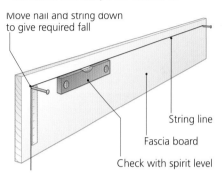

Move nail and string down to give required fall

String line

Fascia board

Check with spirit level

3 Fix a taut string as a guide for positioning the brackets. Fit it as close to the tiles or slates as you can. Run it from the downpipe position to the farthest point of the guttering that will drain into it. This may be at the end of the fascia board or at an angle in the guttering.
   Check with a spirit level that the string is horizontal, and mark its level at the downpipe position with chalk.

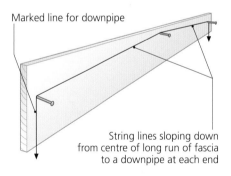

Marked line for downpipe

String lines sloping down from centre of long run of fascia to a downpipe at each end

4 Lower the string at the chalk-mark end by the amount needed to give the correct fall and fix it taut with a nail. The fall should be 15–20mm for every 3m.

5 A long stretch of gutter may have a downpipe at each end. Fix the string line with its highest point in the centre and a fall towards each downpipe. If the outlet is in the middle of a run of gutter, fix string lines at both sides of it.

Fitting the new guttering

1 Screw a bracket in place on the fascia 200mm from the mark at the downpipe position. Align its top with the string line.

2 Screw another bracket in place 150mm from the other end of the run of guttering, aligning it with the string line at the top.

3 Space out brackets equally between these two at intervals of about 500mm.

Alternatively Assemble the gutter on the ground and measure the distance from the centre of the downpipe outlet to the centre of the union piece joining the gutter sections – and from this point to the centre of the next union piece. Mark these distances on the fascia and screw brackets there, aligning their tops with the string. Each join will be supported by a bracket and you can then space out the brackets between at intervals of up to 1m.

4 Clip the gutter, section by section, into the brackets, fitting union pieces where necessary to join the sections. Make sure that the sections are well pressed into place. Lodge the back edge of the gutter under the bracket clip first, then press the front edge down under the other clip.

5 The final section of gutter will have to be cut. Cut it on the ground after measuring off a piece of the right length. If it runs to the end of the fascia, let it extend 50mm beyound the end of the fascia board. Cut it with a hacksaw and smooth the cut with a file.

6 Use either a gutter notching tool or a file to cut notches in the gutter rims for the stopend clips to engage in. Fit the stopend and clip the gutter onto its bracket and into the union piece holding it to the adjoining section.

7 If there is guttering at both sides of the outlet, fit the second run in the same way as the first.

Fitting the new downpipe

1 Measure the length of pipe needed to slope inwards from the gutter outlet to the wall. Cut pipe to this length.

2 Push the offset bends onto the pipe ends and hold this zigzag unit in position at the gutter outlet to test the fit. The lower offset bend should have its outlet the right distance from the wall to accommodate the pipe clip. Saw off more pipe if necessary to achieve the right fit.

3 Clean and wash the pipe ends and the sockets of the bends.

4 With the zigzag section held together again, make a chalk mark along the pipe and onto each offset section to show the correct alignment. Take the unit apart.

5 Apply solvent cement outside the pipe ends and inside the sockets of the bends. Assemble the parts again, lining up the chalk marks.

6 Push the zigzag unit onto the bottom of the gutter outlet.

7 Hold a downpipe section in position over the bottom of the zigzag unit. See whether the top of the downpipe section is in line with a mortar joint. If not, measure how much it needs to be raised.

Saw off this amount plus 10mm from the bottom of the zigzag unit. The extra 10mm leaves a gap to allow for expansion of the pipe in hot weather.

8 Mark, drill and plug holes in the mortar joint to screw the pipe clip into. The distance between the screw holes depends on the type of clip you are using. Hold the clip against the wall to make marks through the holes as guides for drilling.

9 Measure down the chalk mark on the wall to mark the position for drilling holes for the next pipe clip. You may have to cut the bottom end of the section of downpipe to align the clip with a mortar joint. Remember to cut off the extra 10mm again to create an expansion gap inside the socket.

COLLECTING RAINWATER

Position water butts beneath downpipes from the gutters on your house, outbuildings and greenhouse to collect the run-off rainwater from your roofs for use in the garden in times of drought.

Easy-to-install DIY water butts and pipes connect to the guttering system using linking sections that are compatible with the most common drainpipe sizes.

10 At the bottom, cut the pipe so that the shoe will be about 50mm clear of the gully. You may need to lift out the drain grid while you fit the shoe. If the pipe goes direct into the ground, allow enough pipe to do this.

11 Drill and plug holes for brackets between the joints of downpipe sections, spacing them equally not more than 1m apart and aligning them with mortar joints.

12 When all the holes are drilled and plugged, screw the pipe clips in place.

13 If the downpipe goes direct into a gully underground, repair the mortar or other surround.

Re-aligning a gutter

If water forms a pool instead of running away to the downpipe, the fixing screw holding the support bracket or the gutter may be loose.

Remove the screw, tap a wall plug into the screw hole and re-screw the bracket or gutter with a new zinc-plated screw. If, when you check, you find that no screws are loose or, conversely, that several are loose, the fall of the gutter may need correcting. You may have to remove a section of gutter to reach the screws.

Tools *Ladder with a stand-off bracket; hammer; screwdriver; drill with wood bit or high-speed-steel bit, or both; spirit level.*

Materials *Wall plugs; zinc-plated No. 8 or No. 10 screws; two or more 150mm nails; string and nails.*

1 Drive a long, strong nail into the fascia board near each end of the loose section of gutter, immediately below it, to support it. If the loose section is longer than 2m or the gutter is iron, drive in more nails to give it sufficient support.

2 Remove the screws that hold the gutter or its supporting brackets.

3 Fix a taut string line along the length of the fascia board immediately under the guttering. With a spirit level, check it is horizontal then lower the string at the downpipe end to give it a fall towards the downpipe of 15–20mm in every 3m.

4 If the gutter is on brackets, as most gutters are, unscrew those that are letting the gutter sag and move them left or right slightly to new positions so that you can screw into solid wood; make sure the new screw positions align with the string line to give the correct fall.

Alternatively If the gutter is screwed direct to the fascia, raise it to align correctly with the string line and drill new holes through the gutter and into the fascia, about 50mm to the side of the original holes. Refit the gutter using new zinc-plated screws.

Alternatively If the screws through the gutter have been driven into the ends of the roof rafters, not into a fascia board, fix a string line and adjust the position of the screws to bring the gutter to the correct fall. You may have to remove a tile or slate temporarily to reach the screws.

Treating rusted gutters

Treat rust as soon as possible. It contaminates the rainwater and the damage will only increase.

Before you start Make sure you have safety goggles to protect your eyes from flying particles when removing rust. Do not rub the metal too vigorously – it does not have to shine – just remove the rust. If the inside of the gutter cannot be seen from any upstairs window, you can use up left-over gloss paint of any colour instead of buying bitumen paint.

Tools *Ladder with a stand-off bracket; safety goggles; strong work gloves; wire brush or electric drill fitted with wire cup brush or wheel; emery cloth; paintbrush. Perhaps filling knife.*

Materials *Rust-neutralising primer; black bitumen paint or left-over gloss paint. Perhaps roof-and-gutter sealant or glass-fibre filler.*

1 Rub off smaller rust spots with the emery cloth.

2 Remove larger patches of rust with the wire brush or brush wheel fitted in the drill.

3 Apply a coat of rust-neutralising primer to the cleaned parts – and to the rest of the inside of the gutter, if you wish.

4 Seal any small cracks in the gutter with roof-and-gutter sealant.

5 If there is a larger crack or hole, fill it with a glass-fibre filler of the kind used for car body repairs. Be sure to smooth the filling thoroughly so there is no roughness to hold water or silt.

6 Apply a coat of black bitumen or gloss paint. Allow it to dry and apply a second.

Cleaning an overflowing gutter

As fallen leaves can block downpipes and will rot in water butts, gutters should be cleaned out and checked for damage each year in late autumn.

Before you start Wear sturdy work gloves to avoid scraping your hands on rough or rusty edges or on tiles or slates.

Tools *Ladder with a stand-off bracket; protective gloves; small trowel; bucket; piece of hardboard or a large rag. Possibly a hosepipe.*

1 Put the piece of hardboard at the bottom of the downpipe to prevent debris from getting into the gully or the drain, where it could cause a blockage.

Alternatively If the downpipe goes direct into the ground, stuff the rag in the top of it.

2 Scoop out any silt, grit or other debris with the trowel and put it into the bucket. Take care not to let anything drop into the downpipe. Take care not to let any debris fall down the walls because it may cause stains that are hard to remove.

3 Unblock the downpipe and then pour three or four buckets of water slowly into the gutter at the end farthest from the pipe.

Alternatively Use a hosepipe to lead water there. The water should flow quickly and smoothly to the downpipe, leaving the gutter empty.
• If a pool of water remains, the gutter needs re-aligning (page 114).
• If the water leaks through cracks or bad joints, repair the gutter (page 116).
• If the water starts to overflow at the downpipe, the pipe needs cleaning out.

Repairing leaking gutter joints

Walk round the house occasionally during heavy rain to check that all your gutters are working efficiently.

Rainwater dripping through gutters will be washed into drains rather than collected for your use. It also splashes the house walls, causing a water stain on the outside wall and, after a time, moss and algae will grow, disfiguring the wall. If the leak is not cured, damp will penetrate the walls, causing damage indoors.

Leaking metal gutters

A metal gutter is difficult to take apart if the nuts and bolts have corroded, so try to seal the leak by injecting roof-and-gutter sealant into the joint with an applicator gun. First scrape the joint clean and dry it with a hot-air gun. If the leak persists, you will have to dismantle and reseal the joint. Wear strong gloves to protect your hands from rough metal.

Tools *Ladder with a stand-off bracket; gloves; safety goggles; spanner; hammer; wire brush; old chisel; small trowel; paintbrush; narrow-bladed filing knife. Perhaps a junior hacksaw and nail punch.*

Materials *Metal primer; roof-and-gutter sealant; nut and bolt of correct size.*

1 Undo the nut securing the bolt in the joint piece.

Alternatively If the nut will not move, cut through the bolt with a hacksaw and take out the shank with nail punch and hammer.

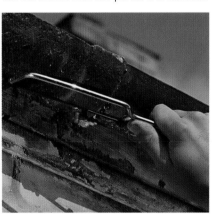

2 Gently hammer the joint piece to separate it from the gutter sections.

3 With the joint dismantled, chisel away the putty and clean rust from the whole joint area with the wire brush. Scoop away the debris with the trowel.

4 Apply a coat of metal primer to the gutter ends and the joint piece and leave it to dry.

5 Spread roof-and-gutter sealant onto the joint piece and reposition the gutter sections on it.

6 Secure the joint with the new nut and bolt.

Leaking plastic gutters

Where pieces of gutter join, or connect with a downpipe, they are clipped to a connector or union piece that has gaskets in it to make the union watertight.

Leakages caused by dirt forcing the seal slightly apart can be cured by cleaning. Squeeze the sides of the gutter inwards to release it from the union piece. If there is no dirt, the gaskets may need renewing.

Tools *Ladder with a stand-off bracket; filling knife.*

Materials *New gaskets or roof-and-gutter sealant.*

1 Squeeze the sides of the gutter sections in order to release them from the clips of the union piece.

2 Gently raise the end of each section of gutter in turn until you can see the gasket in the union piece. Peel the gasket away.

3 Fit the new gaskets, pressing them well into place.

Plastic guttering parts

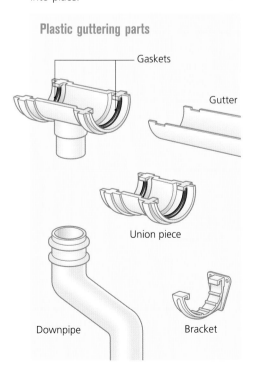

Gaskets

Gutter

Union piece

Downpipe

Bracket

Alternatively Fill the grooves for the gaskets with sealant.

4 Gently squeeze each gutter section in at the sides to ease it back into the union piece clips.

Securing loose downpipes

A downpipe is held to the wall by retaining clips that are screwed into the mortar joints at intervals of about a metre.

If the pipe is not held firmly, it vibrates in strong winds and this can loosen its joints. The sections of downpipe slot loosely one into another; do not seal them together.

Cast-iron pipes

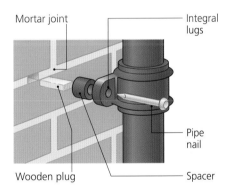

Mortar joint

Integral lugs

Pipe nail

Wooden plug

Spacer

The lugs that hold cast-iron pipes are an integral part of the pipe and are fixed with large nails called pipe nails to wooden plugs inserted in the mortar joints. If only the nails are loose, take them out and fill the hole with wood filler or insert a wall plug into it. Drive the pipe nails back in, or drive in 38mm No. 10 galvanised screws instead.

If the wooden plugs in the wall have come loose or rotted, you will have to remove them and fix new ones.

Tools *Ladder with stand-off bracket; pliers; saw; hammer. Perhaps a screwdriver.*

Materials *Softwood plugs slightly larger than the old ones; wood preservative.*

1 Pull out the old pipe nails with pliers. You can use the nails again if they come out undamaged.

2 Remove the spacers that hold the downpipe away from the wall and keep them on one side.

3 Remove one or more sections of pipe to give access to the plugs. Sections are slotted together. Raise one as high as it will go on the section above to free the lower end from the section below.

4 Take out and discard the plugs.

5 Cut new plugs, sawing and planing or chiselling them until they almost fit the holes. Treat plugs with wood preservative and tap them into place with a hammer.

6 Put back the piece or pieces of downpipe that you have removed.

7 Set the spacers in position behind each pair of lugs and drive the pipe nails through the holes to hold the downpipe securely.

Plastic downpipes

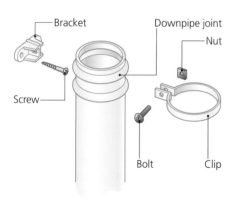

Bracket — Downpipe joint — Nut — Screw — Bolt — Clip

If a plastic downpipe comes loose from the wall, check the screws and the plastic or fibre wall plugs to see if they need renewing to give a better fixing. Use 38mm No. 10 galvanised screws.

It might be easier to move the clip up or down a little to a different mortar joint, and drill and plug new holes to get a firm fixing. Repair the old holes with mortar or exterior filler. Match the colour of the rest of the mortar to make the repair discreet. Do not move a clip fixed at a joint in the downpipe system because it strengthens the joint. You could exchange a one-piece

clip for a two-piece clip, or vice-versa, to give different fixing positions for screws.

Unblocking a downpipe

Rain overflowing from a gutter may be caused by a blocked downpipe, preventing it from draining away.

Before you start Climb up to the gutter and check what is causing the blockage. It could be a ball, a bird's nest or some other object that you can simply lift out from above. But the most likely obstruction is a collection of wind-blown leaves lodged in the mouth of the downpipe.

A pipe with a swan-necked section at the top is more likely to become blocked than a straight downpipe.

Another indication of a blocked downpipe is water seeping out during heavy rain from a joint where sections of downpipe connect. Because the joints are loose, not sealed or glued together, you can tell straight away where the blockage is: it will be in the section immediately below the lowest leaking joint.

Obstructions near the top of the downpipe

If the downpipe is blocked near the top, you can usually clear it by probing with a length of wire. Cover the drain at the bottom of the pipe to prevent any debris from falling into it. Hook out debris if you can; if you cannot, probe until it becomes loose. Flush away remaining loose debris by pouring buckets of water down the pipe or playing a strong jet of water down it from a hose. If the pipe is straight, not swan-necked, tie rags firmly to the end of a stick (such as a bamboo garden cane) to form a ball and push the obstruction loose with it.

Obstructions that are out of reach

Hire a flexible drain rod to clear an obstruction lower down a pipe or in a swan-necked pipe. Or, as a last resort, dismantle the lower part of the downpipe.

Tools *Ladder with a stand-off bracket; screwdriver or pliers or box spanner; long stick. Perhaps a cold chisel and claw hammer.*

1 On a plastic downpipe, remove the screws that hold the pipe clips to the wall. Work from the bottom and remove the screws and clips up to the point it leaks. If the pipe is held by two-part brackets, undo the bolts holding the rings to the back plates; leave the back plates in place. If the pipe is cast-iron, use pliers to pull out the large pipe nails that hold the lugs to the wall. If they are rusted, use a cold chisel and claw hammer to prise the lugs from the wall; keep the nails for re-use.

2 As you free the clips or lugs that hold it, free each section of pipe from the section below and lift it away from the wall.

3 Use a long stick to push out any obstructions inside the sections.

Alternatively Run a garden hose up the pipe to shift any blockage inside.

4 Replace the pipe section by section, working from the top down, and screw or bolt back in place the clips (or nail the lugs) that hold the section to the wall.

Preventing blockages

Wire or plastic covers are sold in different sizes for fitting in the tops of downpipes.
• If there is a hopper at the top of the downpipe, fit fine-mesh wire netting over the top, securing it with fine galvanised wire.
• If there are large deciduous trees nearby, it is worth covering gutters. Lay a strip of plastic netting over a gutter to overlap the top by about 50mm at each side. About every 1m along it, thread a length of twine through the overlaps from the underside of the gutter and tie it firmly to hold the mesh taut. Check the netting surface regularly during autumn; if leaves coat it, rain cannot enter the gutter and will spill over it.

Maintaining gullies

A gully is an underground U-trap that prevents bulky waste from flowing into the drains. It is prone to blockage.

A gully is fitted at the point where a downpipe or waste pipe discharges at ground level, and is then connected to the underground drains. A yard gully is similar but is sited away from the house and collects surface water via an open grating. The trap in the gully is there to collect solid waste material, preventing it from entering the drains and causing a blockage.

In older properties, the water discharges into a gully above a grid fitted over the trap. This grid can become blocked with leaves and other debris, resulting in waste water splashing over the surrounding area.

In newer properties, waste pipes discharge into soil stacks and downpipes discharge into back-inlet gullies. Here the downpipe passes directly through the grating and into the trap, so avoiding over-flow problems. If the gully does not have to act as a yard gully, a screw-down cover provides access to the trap.

Channel gullies taking waste water via a half-round channel are especially prone to grid blockages. Prevent these by putting a cover on the gully. Cut it from outdoor-grade plywood 13–19mm thick. Make a hole for the waste pipe to pass through.

Clearing a blockage

1 Clear all debris from the gully grating. If necessary, prise out the grating and scrub it in hot soapy water.

2 If the blockage is deeper, remove the grating. Wear long rubber gloves or put your arm in a plastic bag. Reach into the trap, which may be up to 600mm deep, and scoop out as much debris as you can.

3 If the obstruction is too solid to scoop out, break it down with a garden trowel.

4 When the gully is cleared, scrub the sides with a nylon pot scourer and hose them down with a fierce jet of water. Disinfect all gloves and tools afterwards.

5 If you cannot find an obstruction in the gully, it may be farther down the drain.

Recycling water in the house and garden

Whether it is collecting rainwater in a butt for watering the garden or in larger quantities for re-use in the house, anything you can do to recycle water will help to preserve valuable drinking water.

Purifying drinking water requires energy and the more water that ends up in our drains the higher the likelihood of flooding from treatment works, resulting in the pollution of rivers and streams. More than that, drinking water is a scarce commodity during prolonged periods of drought, even in a rainy country like Britain and should be treated as such. To ease the demand on piped, purified water, rainwater can be collected and used to water plants, as can the water from your bath or washing. By adjusting your water supply pipes within the home and installing a device to pump water from a tank back into the house, this 'grey' water can also be used to flush the toilet and wash your clothes, but retro-fitting a system like this to an existing house is complicated and expensive.

Water butts

The first place to start as a water-recycler is to install as many water butts as you can around the outside of the house. Fit one at each downpipe from the gutter or, better still if you have room, more than one linked together – a water butt collecting rain from just one slope of a house roof can fill up with one good downpour, leaving the rest of the season's rain to divert into the household drains as before. Don't stop with just the main house roof, either: there will be enough run-off from a garage or even a small garden shed to fill a butt, so fit gutters and downpipes to any roof you can (see pages 110–13).

Choosing a water butt
Water butts come in a variety of styles and sizes from simple black or green plastic cylinders to recycled wooden beer barrels; decorative enamelled metal or plastic butts designed to look like large terracotta urns

are also available, so if your water butt will be in a prominent place you might prefer to seek out one of the more attractive options. Many local councils and water supply companies will subsidise the cost of water butts, although the choices they offer will be limited. To fit a watering can under the tap at the bottom of the butt you will also need a stand for the water butt to sit on and you may need to buy this separately.

If you have children or grandchildren who play in your garden, it is worth choosing a water butt with a childproof lid. These are harder to open than the simplest lids, which just balance on the top of the butt, and are much safer where there is a chance of an inquisitive child climbing up, falling into the water and drowning.

Installation

When you buy a water butt you will also need to buy a kit to link it into your downpipe – this is much easier with plastic downpipes than old iron ones. A rainwater diverter kit contains a section of downpipe which diverts the rain from the downpipe into the water butt and an integral overflow pipe, which takes the water back into the downpipe and to the drain once the water butt is full. To install one of these, position the water butt and decide where in the downpipe the diverter kit needs to be to flow into the top of the butt. Mark the position on the downpipe and use a hacksaw to cut away a slice of downpipe so that the diverter can be slotted in.

Alternatively, stop the downpipe above the level of the water butt and use angled downpipe connectors and short straight sections as necessary to drop the pipe down through a hole in the lid of the butt. Most lids have holes marked for this purpose on the inside and you will need to knock, drill or cut them out. You may need to file the edges of the hole smooth. With

this method, you will need an overflow kit, a narrower bore flexible pipe which fits into the side of the water butt near the top and can be run into a drain or soakaway.

Links and overflows

Overflow kits also allow you to link water butts together. Once the first water butt in the sequence is full, any additional water will flow through the overflow pipe and into the next butt. Remember to fit an overflow into the drain from the last water butt.

WATER BUTT HYGIENE

If you are collecting water solely for watering the garden, it is a good idea to empty and disconnect your water butts over winter, when they will not be needed. Water left sitting in a butt will stagnate and bacteria and silverfish can multiply in it.

Drain the water away, clean the butt thoroughly inside and out and return the rainwater downpipe to discharge temporarily into the drains once more.

While water butts are in use they should always be covered to prevent the growth of algae in the water – which is encouraged by sunlight – as well as to prevent pets, children and small animals falling into the water and drowning.

Using the water from your butt

The simplest way to use your rainwater is by filling a watering can from the tap on the water butt, but if you want to run a hosepipe or need more pressure, then you can buy a small pump. This waterproof device is electric and connects to a length of standard hosepipe. Just connect the hose, drop the pump into the water and turn it on.

Rainwater tanks

If you collect and use a large amount of rainwater it may be worth considering a large tank in place of a number of small water butts. These may be installed on the surface somewhere out of the way or under ground. Metal, plastic or glass fibre tanks are available, or underground ones can be cast in concrete.

To estimate what size of tank to buy, calculate how much rainwater you are likely to collect. Each millimetre of rain that falls on $1m^2$ of roof represents 1 litre of water, so calculate the area of your roof in m^2 and multiply that by the average local annual rainfall, in millimetres.

You probably will not be able to store all the rainfall – and are unlikely to be need to use that much either – but this will give you a guide to the capacity you may need. Remember that you will be drawing water off as well as collecting it, and that the rainfall levels will differ from season to season. For watering the garden, calculate the rainfall from spring to autumn, when you are most likely to need it.

Collecting grey water

Grey water is the waste water from baths, showers, basins and washing machines. With some filtering – more than is required for rainwater – it can be recycled for watering the garden, washing the car, flushing the WC and other jobs where the quality of the water is not critical. Water from washing dishes or other kitchen jobs is not suitable, as it will contain grease and food waste that will encourage bacteria to grow in the collection tank.

In practice, diverting existing waste pipes to run to a grey water collection tank rather than into the main soil stack or drain is expensive and disruptive, so collecting and using grey water is only a viable option for new builds or very dedicated homeowners.

A simple way to recycle this kind of water, particularly during dry summer spells, is to wash dishes by hand in a bowl and to tip the water on the garden afterwards. You could also buy a pump with a hosepipe attachment to empty bathwater directly onto the garden or into a collection tank via an open window.

Using rainwater and grey water in the house

Water collected in large rainwater tanks can be used for flushing a WC or washing clothes, but it must be filtered and allowed to settle first and you will need to install substantial tanks to see you through dry periods. Automatic switch-over systems are available to return to the mains supply if the tank runs dry.

Because collection tanks are so large and heavy once full of water, they are usually buried underground, so they need an electric pump to supply the water to the house. Grey water should not be stored for longer than 24 hours, as it can contain bacteria that may breed, so it is not suitable for collecting in large tanks that will not be emptied on a daily basis.

In an existing property, as with attempting to collect grey water, installing the necessary pipework to recycle collected water throughout the home is a major task. But a separate, dedicated plumbing system could be installed to pipe the water to a single downstairs WC or washing machine in a utility room close to where the tank is located outdoors. The work is likely to be expensive and compared with the savings you may make on your water bill is probably not financially viable, but as an investment in your home and the future you may think it worth while.

Eco-friendly DIY products and suppliers

When you are doing work on your house you may prefer to choose products that are not polluting to the environment in their manufacture or use, or that will help to make your home more energy-efficient. Use this list of contacts to help you.

Decorating and flooring

EarthBorn paints
Brush Mate, Frodsham Business Centre, Bridge Lane, Frodsham, Cheshire WA6 7FZ
Tel: 01928 734171 Fax: 01928 731732
info@earthbornpaints.co.uk
www.earthbornpaints.co.uk

The Alternative Flooring Company Ltd
3b Stephenson Close, East Portway, Andover, Hampshire SP10 3RU
01264 335111
www.alternativeflooring.com

Smile Plastics
(Recycled plastic worktops)
Mansion House, Ford, Shrewsbury, SY5 9LZ
01743 850267
CJW@Smile-Plastics.co.uk
www.smile-plastics.co.uk

The Green Shop
Cheltenham Road, Bisley, Stroud
Gloucestershire, GL6 7BX.
Tel: 01452 770629 Fax: 01452 770104
enquiries@greenshop.co.uk
www.greenshop.co.uk

Building materials and insulation

Association for Environment Conscious Building
PO Box 32, LLandysul, SA44 5ZA
0845 4569773
www.aecb.net

Natural Building Technologies
The Hangar, Worminghall Road, Oakley, Bucks, HP18 9UL
Tel: 01844 338338 Fax: 01844 338525
info@natural-building.co.uk
www.natural-building.co.uk

Centre for Alternative Technology (CAT)
Machynlleth, Powys, SY20 9AZ
01654 705950
www.cat.org.uk

Rounded Developments Enterprises
Sustainable Building Centre, Unit 93, Portmanmoor Road Industrial Estate, Splott, Cardiff, CF24 5HB
029 2040 3399
info@rounded-developments.org.uk
www.rounded-developments.org.uk

Second Nature UK Ltd
(Thermafleece sheep's wool insulation)
Soulands Gate, Soulby, Dacre, Penrith, Cumbria CA11 0JF
Tel: 01768 486285 Fax: 01768 486825
info@secondnatureuk.co.uk
www.secondnatureuk.com

The Green Building Store
Heath House Mill, Heath House Lane, Bolster Moor, West Yorkshire HD7 4JW
Tel: 01484 461705 Fax: 01484 653765
info@greenbuildingstore.co.uk
www.greenbuildingstore.co.uk

FENSA
(Fenestration Self-Assessment Scheme)
www.fensa.org.uk

Glass and Glazing Federation
www.ggf.org.uk

Passivent Ltd
(Natural and energy-efficient ventilation)
2 Brooklands Road, Sale, Cheshire, M33 3SS
0161 962 7113
www.passivent.com

Excel Building Solutions
(Building Products made from sustainable or recycled materials)
Excel Industries Limited, Maerdy Industrial Estate, Rhymney, Gwent NP22 5PY
Tel: 01685 845 200 Fax: 01685 844 106
www.excelfibre.com

Alternative energy sources and water recycling

Rainharvesting Ltd
Unit S2, Inchbrook Trading Estate, Bath
Road, Woodchester, Stroud, GL5 5EY
Tel: 0845 223 5430 Fax: 01453 839260
www.rainharvesting.co.uk

SolarCentury
91–94 Lower Marsh, Waterloo, London
SE1 7AB
Tel: 020 7803 0100 Fax: 020 7803 010
www.solarcentury.co.uk

Greenshop Solar Ltd
Cheltenham Road, Bisley, Stroud,
Gloucestershire GL6 7BX
0845 2235440
enquiries@greenshopsolar.co.uk
www.greenshopsolar.co.uk

Solar Twin Ltd
2nd Floor, 50 Watergate Street, Chester,
CH1 2LA
hi@solartwin.com
www.solartwin.com

Windsave Ltd
27 Woodside Place, Glasgow G3 7QL
0141 353 6841
info@windsave.com
www.windsave.com

British Wind Energy Association
Renewable Energy House, 1 Aztec Row,
Berners Road, London N1 0PW
020 7689 1960
info@bwea.com
www.bwea.com
www.embracewind.com

Plumbing and appliances

Save-a-flush bags
www.save-a-flush.co.uk

Hippo watersavers
P.O Box 110, Ross-on-Wye, Herefordshire
HR9 5YY
Tel: 01989 766667 Fax: 01989 763473
www.hippo-the-watersaver.co.uk

Niagara Corporation Ltd
(Water conservation appliances)
8a Rishworth Street, Wakefield,
West Yorkshire, WF1 3BY
0870 474 017
www.niagaracorp.com

Eco Kettle
Product Creation Ltd.
Contact Peter Ingledew, Design Director
Jasmine House, High Street, Henfield
West Sussex BN5 9HN
01273 494943
pi@productcreation.co.uk
www.ecokettle.com

Safe T Light
Windward House, 34 Hayling Avenue
Portsmouth, Hampshire, PO3 6EA
info@safetlight.co.uk
www.safetlight.co.uk

Monodraught Ltd (Sunpipe)
Halifax House, Cressex Business Park
High Wycombe, Bucks HP12 3SE
01494 897700
info@monodraught.com
www.sunpipe.co.uk

SEDBUK
(Seasonal Efficiency of Domestic Boilers in
United Kingdom – Database)
www.boilers.org.uk

Carbon 300
(Energy-efficient heating & hot water
systems)
100 Haldon Road, Wandsworth, London
SW18 1QQ
Tel: 020 7731 8762
info@carbon300.co.uk
www.carbon300.co.uk

Energy saving organisations

Energy Savings Trust (EST)
21 Dartmouth Street, London SW1H 9BP
020 7222 0101
www.est.org.uk

The Natural Energy Foundation
www.nef.org.uk

Energy Efficiency Advice Centre
Contact your local office on 0800 512012

National Home Energy Rating Scheme
(For a detailed energy audit of your home)
NHER, National Energy Centre, Davy
Avenue, Knowlhill, Milton Keynes,
MK5 8NA
01908 672787
www.nher.co.uk

A,B

appliances
    energy-efficient 17, 18, 92
    scale formation 61
    stand-by mode/switching off 16, 20,
        22, 61
bathrooms
    electricity-saving tips 20-21
    ventilation 20-21, 32
    baths, filling 91, 93
bedrooms: electricity-saving tips 22
boilers 59, 73-74
    back boilers 74
    balanced flue 74
boiler energy management 68
    combination boiler 59, 60, 62, 73
    condensing boilers 12, 74
    conventional boilers 73
    energy rating 73
    open flue 74
    over-heat cut-out 60
    servicing 73
Building Regulations 28, 32

C

cavity wall insulation 10, 14, 29, 32, 50
    dry system 50
    expanding foam insulation 50
central heating 65-69, 82-84
    air in the system 67, 81
    corrosion 67, 81
    draining and refilling the system 55,
        85
    empty rooms/empty house 16, 55
    energy efficiency 16, 60-61
    gravity circulation 59, 82
    installation 65
    leaks 82-84
    open system 58, 85
    pumped system 58
    sealed system 60
    sludge 81, 82
    underfloor heating 70, 72
    see also boilers; radiators
central heating controls 68-69
    programmers 12, 16, 58, 68, 69
    room thermostats 12, 58, 68
Christmas lights 23
clock radios and electric clocks 22
cold water cistern 47, 90, 95
    draining 95
cold-weather checks 55
corrosion and scale inhibitor 67
curtains 14-15, 66

D

dimmer switches 19
dishwashers 92, 93
doors
    draughtproofing 10, 41-42
    porches 41
double glazing 10, 14, 27, 28, 32, 33-37
    replacing 34
    sealed units 33, 34
    secondary glazing 32, 33, 35-37
    triple glazing 33, 39
    uPVC windows 33
downpipes 113, 117-19
    blocked 118-19
    fitting 113
    metal 117
    plastic 118
    securing 117-18
draught excluders 10, 15, 38, 41-42
draughtproofing
    doors 41-42
    floors 43-44
    windows 38-39, 42
draughts, finding source of 40
dry-lined walls 32, 50-53
    fixings 52
dusk-to-dawn lights 22, 23

E,F

electric fires 20
Energy Performance Certificate (EPC) 13, 24
energy ratings in the home 13
expanding foam filler 39
extractor fans 20-21
fan convectors 71
feed-and-expansion cistern 67, 81
floors
    draughtproofing 43-44
floor coverings, laying 43
    gaps below skirting board 44
    insulation 32, 44, 45
    solid 32
    suspended 32, 43-44
    underfloor heating 70, 72
    ventilation 32
frame sealant 38, 39, 40

G

garden: water-saving tips 92-94
gas, advantages of 17
glass, low-emissivity 28, 29, 39
grants 27, 45
grey water 120, 122
gullies 119

guttering 110-19
    blocked 115, 118-19
    downpipes 113, 117-19
    leaking joints 116-17
    metal 115, 116, 117
    plastic 110, 111-13, 116-17
    re-aligning 114-15
    rust 115

H

halls: electricity-saving tips 22-23
hard-water damage 61, 77, 99
HEAT project 45
heating 56-87
    see also central heating; hot water
home energy survey 10-13
home extensions 28-29
Home Information Packs 13
hot water
heating systems 62-64
    secondary hot-water circulation 60
    in summer 69
    waste, avoiding 14, 21, 60-61
    see also hot water; immersion heaters
hot water cylinders 11-12, 62
    built-in insulation 62
    lagging 12, 16, 21, 61, 62
    replacing 75-6
    un-vented cylinders 62
household energy use 15

I,K

immersion heaters 21, 61, 62-63, 69
    replacing 77-79
    thermostats 61, 63, 68, 79
    time switches 61
instantaneous gas heaters 63
instantaneous open-outlook electric
    heaters 63
insulation 30-55
    floors 32, 44, 45
    grants 45
    hot water cylinders 12, 16, 21, 61, 62
    lofts 11, 29, 45, 46-48
    pipes 54-55
    roofs 32, 45, 49
    walls 14, 27, 29, 32, 45, 50-53
    windows 10, 14, 27, 28, 32, 33-39,
        42
isolating valves 96
kettles 18
keyholes 15
kitchens
    electricity-saving 18
    ventilation 32
    water-saving 92

L

lagging
    foam tube 54, 55
    glass-fibre blanket 55
    hot water cylinders 12, 16, 21, 61, 62
    loft-hatch doors 47
    pipes 11, 16, 54-55
    self-adhesive foam wrap 54, 55
laundry
    drying 17
    washing 17, 93
letterboxes 41
light bulbs, low-energy 11, 13, 16, 19,
      23, 27
lights
    Christmas lights 23
    dimmer switches 19
    dusk-to-dawn lights 22, 23
    halogen spotlights 19
    low-level lighting 19, 20
    motion-sensitive light switches 21
    night lights 22, 23
    security lights 23
    solar-powered light circuit 25
    timer switches 23
    turning off 19
liquefied petroleum gas (LPG) 81
living rooms: electricity-saving 20
loft insulation 11, 29, 45, 46-48
    blanket rolls 46-47, 48
    expanded polystyrene sheets 48
    loose-fill insulation 47, 48
    mineral fibre batts 48
    quantities 48
    reflective foil building paper 48
lofts 46-48
    conversions 28, 32
loft-hatch doors, lagging 47
    vapour barriers 46, 48
    ventilation 11, 32, 47

M,N,O,P

magnetic water conditioner 61
microwave ovens 18
night lights 22, 23
off-peak electricity 20, 61
ovens 18
pipes
    boxing in 87
    burst pipe repairs 97
    hot water pipes 60
    insulation 54-55
    lagging 11, 16
    leaks 82, 94
    scale formation 61
planning permission 29
porches 41
protective clothing 46

R

radiant heaters 20
radiators 70
    balancing a radiator circuit 80-81
    bleeding 67, 81, 82
    faults 81-82
    leaks 82-84
    positioning 66, 87
    removing and replacing 86-87
    sizing 71
    thermostatic radiator valves (TRVs) 12, 20, 68, 83, 84, 87
    valves, replacing 84
rainwater tanks 28, 122
recycling water 120-2
refridgerators 17
rising main, draining 95
roofs
    flat 32, 49
    insulation 32, 45, 49
    pitched 32
    spray-on insulation 45
    see also lofts

S

Safe-T-Light 23
scale formation 61, 77, 99
security lights 23
showers 60, 93
    power showers 91
shower heads, aerated 28, 91
shower-diverters 104
    water-saving tips 91
skirting heaters 70
solar power 24-26
    energy capacity 25-26, 64
    set-up costs 24, 64
    solar panels 13, 24-25, 29
solar water heating 64
sprinklers, garden 93, 94
stoptaps 95-96
    jammed 96
storage heaters (room heaters) 20
storage heaters (water heaters) 63
    cistern-type 63
    low-pressure type 63
sun rooms and glass extensions 28-29

T

taps 98-104
    aerated 28, 91
    ceramic discs 98, 101
    dripping 55, 91, 99-104
    hard-water damage 99
    mixer taps 91, 103-4
    O-rings 103-4

    spindle taps 98, 99, 101, 102
    stoptap 95-96
tap conversion kits 100
thermal board 50
thermostats
    immersion heaters 61, 63, 68, 79
    room thermostats 12, 58, 68
trench-duct heaters 70
tumble driers 17

U,V

U values 28, 33
ventilation 11, 32, 47

W

walls
    cavity walls 10, 14, 29, 32, 50
    dry-lining 32, 50-53
    external insulation 32
    insulation 14, 27, 29, 32, 45, 50-53
    solid walls 10-11, 14, 32, 50
Warm Front scheme 27
washing machines 92, 93
water
    cutting off the water supply 95-96
    household consumption 93
    saving 88-122
water butts 28, 93, 113, 120-2
water meters 90
water rate rebates 120
water softeners 61
WCs 93, 105-9
    close-coupled WC 106-7
    composting toilet 90
    dual-flush 28, 90
    faulty cistern 108-9
    flushing problems 108
    pan joints 106
    replacing 105-7
water-saving tips 90
wind turbines 24, 26, 29
windows
    casement windows 38, 42
    cracked windows 37
    draught excluders 10
    draughtproofing 38-39, 42
    gaps around window frame 39-40
    sash windows 38, 42
    single-glazed 10
    see also double glazing

Acknowledgments

All images in this book are copyright of the Reader's Digest Association Limited, with the exception of those in the following list.

The position of photographs and illustrations on each page is indicated by letters after the page number:
T = Top; **B** = Bottom; **L** = Left; **R** = Right; **C** = Centre

The majority of images in this book are © Reader's Digest and were previously published in Reader's Digest *DIY Manual*.

Front cover (House) arcblue.com/© Peter Durant
Back cover Alamy Images/© Brian Nesbitt
1 iStockphoto.com/Audrey Chmelyor
2 iStockphoto.com/Khanh Trang **12** iStockphoto.com/Gordon Ball **14** iStockphoto.com/Andrejs Pidjass
15 T iStockphoto.com/Alan Egginton
16 T iStockphoto.com/L-Glass **BL** iStockphoto.com/Fred Dimmock **BR** iStockphoto.com/Nick Schlax
17 T iStockphoto.com/Diane Diederich
18L www.ecokettle.com **R** iStockphoto.com/Israel Talby **19** Alamy Images/Sylvia Cordaiy
20 Stephen Chiang **21** Monodraught www.sunpipe.co.uk

22 B iStockphoto.com/Eva Serrabassa
T Alamy Images/© Photofusion **23 T** Alvey & Towers Picture Library **B** www.safetlight.co.uk 01483765252
24 iStockphoto.com/photovoltaic
25 iStockphoto.com/Otmar Smit **26** Alamy Images/© Paul Glendell **30-31** iStockphoto.com/Branko Miokovic **45** Ecoscene/©Chirich Gryniewicz
56-57 iStockphoto.com **64** Alamy Images/© Paul Glendell **70 R, BL, BR** www.bisque.co.uk
71 Myson Radiators **88-89** iStockphoto.com/Duncan Walker **91** iStockphoto.com **T** © Aqualisa/Alexandra Broad Associates **B** Alamy Images/© Trevor Payne
92 T © Comma Image **93 B** Alamy Images/© Rob Walls **94 L** iStockphoto.com/leefoster
R Alamy Images/© The Garden Picture Library
121 L Alamy Images/© Mark Boulton
122 Alamy Images/© Brian Nesbitt

Reader's Digest Energy-Efficient Home Manual is based on material in *Reader's Digest DIY Manual*, published by The Reader's Digest Association Limited, London.

First Edition Copyright © 2007
The Reader's Digest Association Limited,
11 Westferry Circus, Canary Wharf,
London E14 4HE
www.readersdigest.co.uk

Editor Alison Candlin

Art Editor Louise Turpin

Assistant Editor Diane Cross

Editorial Consultant Mike Lawrence

Proofreader Ron Pankhurst

Indexer Marie Lorimer

Reader's Digest General Books

Editorial Director Julian Browne

Art Director Anne-Marie Bulat

Managing Editor Alastair Holmes

Head of Book Development Sarah Bloxham

Picture Resource Manager Sarah Stewart-Richardson

Pre-press Account Managers Penny Grose and Sandra Fuller

Senior Production Controller Deborah Trott

Product Production Manager Claudette Bramble

Origination Colour Systems Limited, London
Printed and bound in China by CT Printing

ISBN: 978 0 276 44258 2
BOOK CODE: 400-352 UP0000-1
ORACLE CODE: 250011349S.00.24